TEMPTING TREATS

Chocolate

I dedicate this book to Richard for his love, support and calm while all around was chaos.

TEMPTING TREATS

Chocolate

Janice Murfitt

OVER 100 IRRESISTIBLE CHOCOLATE IDEAS

LITTLE, BROWN AND COMPANY

A Little Brown Book
© Little, Brown & Company 1992

First published in Great Britain in 1989
by Macdonald & Co (Publishers) Ltd
This edition reprinted by Little, Brown 1992

British Library Cataloguing in Publication Data
Murfitt, Janice
  Chocolate,
  I. Food : Dishes using choclate – Recipes
  I. Title
  641.6374

ISBN 0 316 90617 4

Typeset by Bookworm Typesetting Manchester
Printed and bound by Imago Publishing Ltd.

Senior Editor: Joanna Lorenz
Art Director: Linda Cole
Art Editor: Muffy Dodson
Designer: Ingrid Mason
Photographer: Alan Newnham

Little, Brown and Company
165 Great Dover Street
London
SE1 4YA

CONTENTS

INTRODUCTION

Chocolate is sheer luxury; indulgent and sophisticated, its smooth, rich and intense flavour can be appreciated in many ways and will transform the simplest ingredients into a recipe of distinction. A versatile medium, it offers a great variety of flavours, textures and colours.

All the recipes in this book use confectioner's and eating chocolate, and bakers' compounds. Unless a recipe states a definite type of chocolate, the choice is yours. A good guide is to use any chocolate for baking, but when melted chocolate is used as a final finish, use a good quality chocolate simply for flavour and appearance.

Choosing the Right Chocolate

There are basically three types of chocolate: couverture, confectioner's or baker's, and eating chocolate. All three are obtainable as plain, milk and white chocolate.

Couverture is the finest and most expensive chocolate used for confectionery. It contains all cocoa butter, a very hard fat which produces chocolate of the best flavour and texture. When used, it must be tempered first to obtain high gloss and hard texture.

Tempering chocolate is a very exacting process; cocoa butter is an unstable substance made up of a number of individual fats that melt at different temperatures. To be melted, it has to be heated and cooled to different temperatures before successfully using, so it is best left to the professional.

Couverture chocolate is obtainable from specialized sugarcraft and confectioners' shops.

Confectioner's chocolate is a simplified couverture with some of the hard cocoa butter replaced with a soft vegetable or nut fat. This makes the chocolate easier to work with: it melts at one temperature and liquifies enough to be used for coating and dipping as well as all types of cooking. A good quality confectioner's, dipping or easy chocolate has a good flavour and texture.

Baker's can no longer be called 'chocolate' because the quantity of replacement fat is higher than cocoa butter, so it is referred to as 'chocolate flavour covering'. It is less expensive than real chocolate, and being a good all-round cooking product it may be used for all the recipes in the book – but keep in mind that the flavour is not so good as real chocolate.

Eating chocolate has a wonderful flavour and texture. It is made from a moderate amount of cocoa butter mixed with other fats and additives.

Eating chocolate is ideal for desserts, cakes, biscuits, icings and decorations. When melted, it remains thick, but piped from a small bag it can be used for decorating and will set hard. It is not suitable for dipping and coating unless butter, milk or cream are added to thin the chocolate to keep it soft.

Plain, Milk and White Chocolate

Plain chocolate is made from a mixture of cocoa powder, chocolate liquor, cocoa butter, some other fats, and sugar. The more chocolate liquor and cocoa butter used proportionally to sugar, the darker and richer the chocolate.

Milk chocolate is a mixture of cocoa powder, chocolate liquor, cocoa butter and other fats, sugar, milk and sometimes cream. The milk dilutes the chocolate liquor, giving a mild flavour to the chocolate and making a lighter coloured, softer, sweet chocolate.

White chocolate is made from pale yellow cocoa butter, other fats, sugar and milk. This produces a soft, sweet white chocolate that when melted is thin enough for coating and dipping.

Other Chocolate Products

Cocoa and unsweetened chocolate powder can be used for baking, sifting, coating and drinks.

Drinking chocolate is a mixture of cocoa and sugar. It can be used for cooking and for drinks.

Chocolate spread is a mixture of fat-reduced cocoa and sugar syrup. It is useful for drizzling over ice cream or topping cakes and pastries.

Chocolate hazelnut spread is a mixture of cocoa fats, sugar and hazelnuts. It is ideal for spreading as an icing on cakes, or for piping into quick decorations.

Working with Chocolate

Chocolate should always be used as fresh as possible; wrap any leftovers in foil or cling film to prevent absorption of other flavours and smells. Always store in a dry, cool place; if chocolate becomes too warm, it will become streaked or covered in a white fat bloom. Never store chocolate for more than a few months before using as the flavour begins to deteriorate.

Melting Chocolate

Break chocolate into small pieces and place in a large, dry, clean bowl over a pan of *hand-hot* water. Ensure base of bowl does not touch water. Do not beat, but stir occasionally until completely melted; this you cannot hurry and the chocolate temperature should not exceed 100–110°F (38–43°C), otherwise when it eventually sets, the surface will be covered with a white fat bloom.

Never allow moisture, steam or condensation to come into contact with the chocolate or it will become thick and unusable.

Leave the bowl over water during use, unless you require the chocolate to become thicker. Any leftover chocolate can always be re-used so there is no waste.

Using Melted Chocolate

Coating. Stand cakes, sweets or biscuits on a fine cooling rack, spaced a little apart. Place a large piece of bakewell underneath to catch excess chocolate. Depending on size of piece being coated, use a ladle full of enough chocolate to coat the whole area in one go.

Pour quickly, allow excess to fall, and tap tray to level chocolate. Repeat with another layer after the first one has set, if liked. Return fallen chocolate from bakewell back into bowl.

Dipping. Have everything ready before starting; all items to be dipped should be at room temperature, otherwise the chocolate will set before smoothly coating. Use confectioner's dipping forks or large dinner forks and have several sheets of bakewell ready to take the dipped items.

Place items individually into chocolate, and turn once with dipping fork to coat evenly. Lift out with fork, tap gently on side of bowl to remove excess chocolate, then place onto paper. Mark or decorate top and leave to set.

Spreading. Spoon melted chocolate onto surface to be covered using a palette knife to paddle chocolate backwards and forwards to cover surface. Mark with lines or swirls as chocolate sets.

Piping chocolate. There are easy ways of piping chocolate. One is to use chocolate hazelnut spread, which is the ideal consistency. Placed in a greaseproof paper piping bag fitted with a small star nozzle, borders of shells, stars or whirls may be piped.

Melted chocolate is more difficult to pipe through a metal nozzle as the coldness of the metal sets the chocolate before you start. Add a few drops of glycerine to the chocolate to thicken it, rather than allowing the chocolate to cool and thicken, then pipe through a nozzle as quickly as possible. If the chocolate does start to set, warm the nozzle in your hands.

To pipe threads or lines of chocolate, use a greaseproof paper piping bag and snip off the point to the size of the hole required.

Colouring. To colour white chocolate, use oil-based or powder food colourings, as any liquids added to chocolate will cause it to thicken and become unusable.

Note on Recipes

The recipes in this book are for small sized items – adjust as necessary for larger servings. Follow either the metric or imperial quantities given in any recipe, but not a mixture of the two.

Chill & Cut

No skills are required to master the art of chocolate chill and cut recipes – the ingredients are just mixed together and refrigerated.

This chapter has been designed with a busy lifestyle in mind. All the recipes are simple amalgamations of interesting ingredients that produce quick and scrumptious goodies. There are gâteaux and desserts for special occasions, everyday cakes and cookie bars, and quick lunch-box fillers.

No cooking is required other than melting the chocolate, and no special techniques are involved except the occasional whizzing of ingredients in a food processor.

It is a good idea to make up several recipes and keep them in the refrigerator, ready to cut into servings as and when required. Dress them up with pretty decorations of fruit zest twists, sugar-frosted flowers, or chocolate curls and cut-outs.

Most of the recipes have been made in everyday-sized tins, but this is very flexible as there is no cooking involved. For instance, Richard's chocolate cake (aptly named as it is his favourite recipe) can be made in tiny loaf tins instead of one large tin; serve individually instead of in slices.

CHOCOLATE NUT TORTE

Makes 8

2oz (50g) almonds
2oz (50g) skinned
   hazelnuts
4floz (100ml) milk
3oz (75g) unsalted
   butter
3oz (75g) icing sugar,
   sieved
2 egg yolks
4oz (100g) plain
   chocolate, melted
24 sponge fingers
2 tbsp sherry
1/4pt (150ml) cream,
   whipped
chocolate curls (p.144)
   to decorate

Toast nuts until golden brown, grind finely and place in a bowl. Bring milk to boil, pour over nuts and leave until cold and thick.

Cream butter and icing sugar in a bowl until fluffy. Beat in egg yolks and chocolate, then stir into nut mixture.

Line a 1lb (450g) loaf tin with foil. Dip 8 sponge fingers quickly in sherry and arrange in base of tin. Spread with ½ chocolate mixture. Repeat to make 3 layers of sponge fingers and 2 layers of filling. Press well down, cover with foil and chill for several hours.

Turn out, spread top and sides with cream, and decorate with piped cream and chocolate curls. Chill until ready to serve. Cut into 8 slices.

BRANDY BUTTER ROLLS

Makes 16

BRANDY BUTTER ICING

2oz (50g) unsalted butter
4oz (100g) icing sugar, sieved
1 tbsp brandy

BISCUIT BASE

1 tbsp caster sugar
7oz (200g) digestive biscuit crumbs
3oz (75g) plain cake crumbs
8oz (225g) plain chocolate, melted
water, to mix

Beat butter, icing sugar and brandy together in a bowl until fluffy. Cut a 10" (25cm) square of foil and sprinkle with caster sugar.

Stir biscuit and cake crumbs into chocolate and mix to a firm dough, adding water if necessary.

Put dough on foil and roll out thinly to an 8" (20cm) square. Spread evenly with butter icing and roll into a firm roll. Wrap in foil, chill until firm, then cut into ½" (1cm) thin slices as required.

AMARETTI SWEETMEATS

Makes 20

1oz (25g) ground
  almonds
7oz (200g) petit beurre
  biscuits, crushed
6oz (175g) amaretti or
  ratafia, crushed
6oz (175g) plain
  chocolate
4oz (100g) unsalted
  butter
2 tbsp clear honey

Mix together almonds, biscuits and 4oz (100g) of amaretti in a bowl.

Melt chocolate and butter in a pan, stir over gentle heat, then remove. Stir in honey. Pour into biscuit mixture, and stir until well blended.

Place mixture on a 12" (30cm) length of foil and shape into a 10" (25cm) roll. Wrap up firmly and chill for 1 hour.

Unwrap, and roll in remaining crushed amaretti to coat. Cut into ½" (1cm) thin slices to serve.

CHOCOLATE CHESTNUT APPLE CAKE

Makes 10

15½oz (440g) can
  unsweetened
  chestnut purée
¼pt (150ml) apple
  purée
4oz (100g) plain
  chocolate, melted
30 sponge fingers
3 tbsp sherry
¼pt (150ml) cream,
  whipped
chocolate cut-out
  triangles (p.149) to
  decorate

Place chestnut purée, apple purée and melted chocolate in a food processor. Blend evenly until smooth.

Dip 10 sponge fingers quickly into sherry; arrange in a row on a serving plate. Spread with ⅓ chocolate filling. Repeat to make 3 layers of sponge fingers and 2 filling layers.

Mix together ⅔ remaining filling with cream. Spread top and sides evenly, then pipe remaining filling around top of cake. Decorate with chocolate cut-outs and chill until required. Cut into 10 slices.

CORNFLAKE CRACKLES

Makes 15

2oz (50g) butter
2oz (50g) icing sugar,
  sieved
2oz (50g) golden syrup
2 tbsp cocoa
2oz (50g) cornflakes
2oz (50g) banana
  chips, crushed
2oz (50g) pine nuts
2oz (50g) glacé
  cherries, chopped

Melt butter, icing sugar, syrup and cocoa in a pan, stir over gentle heat, then remove. Add cornflakes, banana chips, pine nuts and cherries, and stir until well mixed.

Divide mixture between 15 paper cake cases and chill until firm.

GINGER LEMON CHEESE CRUNCH

Makes 8

GINGER BASE
1oz (25g) butter
2oz (50g) plain
  chocolate, melted
7oz (200g) gingernut
  biscuits, crushed
2 tbsp golden syrup

FILLING
7oz (200g) condensed
  milk
4oz (100g) white
  chocolate, melted
finely grated rind 2
  lemons
4 tbsp lemon juice
1/4pt (150ml) double
  cream, whipped
chocolate curls (p.144)
  to decorate

Melt butter and chocolate in a pan, stir over gentle heat, then remove. Stir in biscuits and syrup until well mixed. Press mixture evenly over base and sides of 8 3" (7.5cm) fluted tart tins.

Add condensed milk to white chocolate, stir until smooth, then stir in lemon rind and juice. Leave until thickened.

Fill each biscuit case and chill until set. Decorate with piped cream and grated chocolate curls.

MUESLI BARS

Makes 12

2oz (50g) butter
2oz (50g) clear honey
4oz (100g) milk
  chocolate
2oz (50g) wheat flakes
3oz (75g) rolled oats,
  toasted
1oz (25g) dried apple
  slices, chopped
1oz (25g) peanut
  kernels, chopped
6 dried apricots,
  chopped
2 dried figs, chopped

TOPPING
3 tbsp chocolate spread
2 dried apricots,
  chopped
2 tsp chopped peanut
  kernels

Melt butter, honey and chocolate in a pan, stir over gentle heat, then remove. Add all remaining ingredients and mix until well blended.

Press mixture evenly in a buttered 14x4½" (35x11cm) fluted tin and chill for 1 hour.

Turn out of tin, spread top with chocolate spread and sprinkle with fruit and nuts. Cut into 12 bars.

MARASCHINO CRUNCH

Makes 12

BISCUIT BASE
*4oz (100g) milk
   chocolate*
2oz (50g) butter
2oz (50g) golden syrup
*7oz (200g) rich tea
   biscuits, crushed*

*3oz (75g) maraschino
   cherries, chopped*

TOPPING
*3oz (75g) milk
   chocolate, melted*
12 split almonds
*6 maraschino cherries,
   halved*

Melt chocolate, butter and syrup in a pan, stir over gentle heat, then remove. Add biscuits and cherries, and stir until well mixed. Spread mixture evenly into an 8" (20cm) fluted flan tin and chill for 1 hour.

   Remove crunch from tin. Spread top with milk chocolate and arrange almonds and cherries on top. When set, cut into 12 wedges.

TROPICAL COCONUT BITES

Makes 16

2oz (50g) crystallized
papaya pieces
2oz (50g) crystallized
pineapple pieces
1 tbsp lemon juice
2 tbsp evaporated milk

3oz (75g) plain or
white chocolate,
melted
5oz (150g) desiccated
coconut
1oz (25g) white
chocolate, grated

Soak papaya and pineapple in lemon juice for 15 minutes to soften.

Stir evaporated milk into plain or white chocolate. Add coconut and soaked fruit, and mix well together.

Shape mixture into 16 small balls and roll each in grated chocolate to coat. Chill for ½ hour.

RICHARD'S CHOCOLATE CAKE

Makes 16

CHOCOLATE ICING
4oz (100g) plain
  chocolate
2oz (50g) butter
1 egg, beaten
6oz (175g) icing sugar,
  sieved
piped white chocolate
  pieces (p.154) to
  decorate

CAKE
3oz (75g) butter
4 tbsp golden syrup
4 tbsp drinking
  chocolate
2oz (50g) glacé
  cherries, chopped
2oz (50g) dried
  apricots, chopped
2oz (50g) chopped
  hazelnuts, toasted
7oz (200g) petit beurre
  biscuits, crushed

Melt chocolate and butter in a bowl over a pan of hot water. Stir in egg, add icing sugar and beat well. Cool.

Melt butter, syrup and drinking chocolate in a pan, stir over gentle heat, then remove. Add all remaining cake ingredients and mix well together.

Line a 1lb (450g) loaf tin with foil, press in ½ biscuit mixture evenly and spread with ⅓ chocolate icing. Top with remaining biscuit mixture, level top, cover and chill for 1 hour.

Invert cake onto a board, remove foil and spread sides with another ⅓ chocolate icing. Pipe remaining icing on top of cake and decorate with chocolate pieces. Cut in ½" (1cm) slices.

WHITE CHOCOLATE POPS

Makes 18

1 tbsp vegetable oil
1 ¹/₂oz (40g) popping corn
2 tbsp sesame seeds
2 tbsp desiccated coconut
4oz (100g) white chocolate, melted
2 tbsp chopped glacé fruit to decorate

Heat oil in a large pan, add corn, cover and cook until corn has stopped popping. Place in a bowl with sesame seeds and coconut, and mix well. Stir in chocolate until evenly mixed.

Divide mixture between 18 paper cake cases. Sprinkle glacé fruit on top of each and chill until set.

TOFFEE ORANGE CRISPS

Makes 20

*6oz (175g) vanilla
   toffee
2 tbsp orange juice
3oz (75g) orange-
   flavoured chocolate
3oz (75g) rice crispies
orange rind spirals to
   decorate*

Melt toffee and orange juice in a pan, stir over gentle heat, then remove. Add chocolate; allow to melt. Stir in rice crispies until evenly coated.

Press mixture evenly into a bakewell-lined 11x7" (28x17.5cm) swiss roll tin. Chill until firm. Cut into 20 diamonds. Decorate with spirals of orange rind.

STRAWBERRY CHEESE SLICES

Makes 10

8oz (225g)
    philadelphia soft
    cheese
8oz (225g) Greek
    yogurt
4 tbsp orange juice
1 tsp finely grated
    orange rind
6oz (175g) white
    chocolate, melted
36 (2 packets) tea
    finger biscuits
12oz (350g)
    strawberries, sliced

Mix together cheese, yogurt, 2 tbsp of orange juice and rind in a bowl until well blended. Stir in chocolate.

Dip 9 biscuits quickly in remaining orange juice and arrange in an oblong (3 biscuits wide and 3 biscuits long) on a serving plate. Spread with ¼ filling and top with ¼ strawberry slices. Repeat to make 4 biscuit layers and 3 filling layers.

Cover top and sides of cake evenly with filling. Pipe remaining filling around top edge of cake. Decorate with remaining strawberries. Chill until ready to serve; cut into 10 slices.

CARIBBEAN SLICES

7³/₄oz (220g) can
    pineapple rings
4oz (100g) cream
    cheese
2¹/₂oz (60g) carton
    pineapple fromage
    frais
2oz (50g) white
    chocolate, melted
8oz (225g) gingernut
    biscuits
TOPPING
2 tsp cocoa
¹/₄pt (150ml) double
    cream
white chocolate curls
    (p.144) to decorate

Strain pineapple juice into a bowl and chop pineapple finely. Beat cream cheese and fromage frais and white chocolate in a bowl until fluffy. Stir in ½ chopped pineapple.

Dip each biscuit quickly in pineapple juice, then sandwich together in pairs with cheese mixture.

Arrange biscuit pairs in a long roll, spreading remaining cheese mixture in between each to join up roll. Wrap in foil and chill for several hours or overnight.

Mix together cocoa and cream; stir occasionally until beginning to set. Unwrap roll, spread with chocolate cream and decorate with chocolate curls. Slice on the slant for a layered effect.

Biscuits & Cookies

*Smart or plain, crunchy or soft,
here is a range of chocolate biscuits
and cookies to suit all occasions.*

It is a lovely thing to be able to offer home-made biscuits and cookies to guests and children. Although biscuits are not often termed as healthy eating, I have tried to keep sugar to a minimum and use lots of health-giving ingredients such as wholemeal flour, nuts, dried fruits, honey and citrus zest and juice.

A great variety is included here, from individually piped biscuits (using a biscuit machine or piping bag and nozzle), to simple chill and cut cookies. It is useful to make some of the recipes in large tins so they can be cut up as and when required, like the chocolate crunch bars, apricot oat jacks or shortbreads.

Other special recipes that are very versatile are the chocolate rum snaps and stripy cigarettes, which can be served with ice cream or desserts or even made in basket shapes to hold the ice cream – a very pretty effect.

For lunch box fillers or biscuits and cookies to have with tea or coffee, try the palmiers, pretzels, cherry oat chips, florentines and chocolate gems, which look as though they have been iced but are in fact piped with coloured white chocolate.

CHOCOLATE FANCIES

Makes 40

DOUGH
4oz (100g) butter
2oz (50g) caster sugar
1 egg
1 tsp vanilla essence
7oz (200g) plain flour
1oz (25g) cornflour

TOPPING
6oz (175g) white
    chocolate, melted
6oz (175g) plain
    confectioner's
    chocolate, melted

Cream butter and sugar together in a bowl until fluffy; beat in egg and vanilla essence. Sieve in flour and cornflour, and mix to a soft dough. Wrap in cling film and chill for ½ hour.

Roll out dough to ⅛" (2mm) thick and cut out 40 shapes with fancy biscuit cutters, re-rolling dough when necessary.

Arrange on buttered baking sheets and bake in a preheated 350°F/180°C/Gas 4 oven for 15 minutes until lightly browned. Cool.

Dip some biscuits in white chocolate, some in plain chocolate and some in half white, half plain. Place on bakewell to set. Then, pipe beads or lines of contrasting chocolate on each biscuit.

APRICOT OAT JACKS

Makes 16

4 tbsp clear honey
3oz (75g) butter
2oz (50g) light soft
  brown sugar
2oz (50g) plain
  chocolate
5oz (150g) rolled oats

1oz (25g) desiccated
  coconut
1oz (25g) sesame
  seeds
2oz (50g) dried
  apricots, chopped
2–3 apricots, chopped,
  to decorate

Melt honey, butter, sugar in a pan, stir over gentle heat, then remove. Add chocolate; leave to melt. Mix in oats, coconut, sesame seeds and apricots well.

Line a 7″ (17.5cm) square shallow tin with bakewell. Spread oat mixture into tin and level top. Bake in a preheated 350°F/180°C/Gas 4 oven for 20–25 minutes until golden brown and firm to touch.

Cool in tin, turn onto a wire rack and mark into 16 squares with a sharp knife. Decorate with chopped apricot.

CHERRY OAT CHIPS

Makes 30

4oz (100g) butter,
  softened
2oz (50g) caster sugar
5oz (150g) plain flour
1oz (25g) rice flour
½oz (15g) cocoa

1 egg
1½oz (40g) milk
  chocolate dots

TOPPING
1½oz (40g) rolled oats
15 glacé cherries,
  halved

Put all dough ingredients into a bowl. Beat to form a soft dough.

Take 30 tsp mixture and form each into a smooth ball; toss in oats to coat and place apart on bakewell-lined baking sheets.

Press each ball flat and top with a cherry half. Bake in a preheated 350°F/180°C/Gas 4 oven for 10–15 minutes. Cool.

CHOCOLATE CHIP SHORTBREAD

Makes 12

4oz (100g) plain flour
2oz (50g) ground rice
1oz (25g) caster sugar
4oz (100g) unsalted
  butter
2oz (50g) milk
  chocolate dots

Sieve flour, ground rice and sugar into a bowl. Rub in butter until mixture begins to form coarse crumbs. Add ¾ chocolate dots; knead into a soft dough.

Roll out and cut into 12 2″ (5cm) fluted rounds and place on a buttered baking sheet. Decorate with remaining chocolate dots.

Bake in a preheated 325°F/170°C/Gas 3 oven for 20–30 minutes until lightly browned. Cool on baking sheet, then loosen with a palette knife.

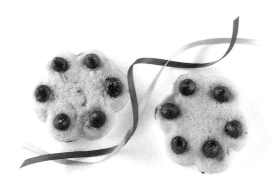

CHOCOLATE GEMS

Makes 30

3oz (75g) plain flour
1oz (25g) caster sugar
2oz (50g) butter
1oz (25g) plain
   chocolate, melted

TOPPING
6oz (175g) white
   chocolate, melted
pink, yellow and green
   oil-based or powder
   food colours

Sieve flour and sugar into a bowl, and rub in butter until mixture begins to form coarse crumbs. Add plain chocolate and knead to a soft dough. Roll out to ¼" (5mm) thick.

Using a ¾" (2cm) fluted cocktail cutter, cut out 30 shapes. Arrange on bakewell-lined baking sheets and bake in a preheated 350°F/180°C/Gas 4 oven for 15 minutes. Cool.

Divide chocolate between 3 bowls and tint pale pink, yellow and green with food colours.

Fit a piping bag with a small star nozzle. When chocolate is thick, fill bag with one colour at a time and pipe stars on ⅓ of biscuits. Repeat with remaining colours and leave to set.

CHOCOLATE PINE TUILLES

Makes 24

2 egg whites
4oz (100g) icing sugar,
  sieved
2oz (50g) plain flour
2oz (50g) butter,
  melted
2oz (50g) plain
  chocolate, grated
2oz (50g) pine nuts
icing sugar to dust

Whisk egg whites in a bowl until stiff. Whisk in icing sugar, flour and butter until smooth. Place mixture in a nylon piping bag with a ¼" (5mm) plain nozzle.

Line 3 baking sheets with bakewell. Draw 4 3½" (8.5cm) circles on each, and invert paper. Pipe or spoon small rounds of mixture onto each circle, and spread thinly to edges. Sprinkle with grated chocolate and pine nuts.

Bake one sheet at a time in a preheated 400°F/200°C/Gas 6 oven for 3–4 minutes until golden at edges. Loosen each tuille and quickly mould over a rolling pin to set (a few seconds). Cool on wire rack and repeat until all tuilles are baked and moulded. Sift with icing sugar and store in an airtight container.

CHOCOLATE PRETZELS

Makes 40

4oz (100g) butter
4oz (100g) light soft
  brown sugar
1 egg, beaten
4oz (100g) plain
  chocolate, melted

9oz (275g) self-raising
  wholemeal flour

TOPPING
1 egg white, whisked
1oz (25g) white
  chocolate, grated
icing sugar (optional)

Cream butter and sugar in a bowl until fluffy; beat in egg and chocolate until evenly blended. Sieve in flour, and mix to form a soft dough. Cling film and chill.

Break off walnut-sized pieces of dough and roll into 40 10″ (25cm) thin lengths. To shape pretzels, pick up ends of each dough length, form a loop, cross ends over, take ends back and press in position at top of loop. Place on a baking sheet lined with bakewell, and repeat. Chill for ½ hour.

Bake in a preheated 350°F/180°C/Gas 4 oven for 15–20 minutes. Brush with egg white and sprinkle with chocolate, or sift with icing sugar.

CHOCOLATE RUM SNAPS

Makes 20

2oz (50g) unsalted
   butter
2oz (50g) caster sugar
2oz (50g) golden syrup
1oz (25g) plain
   chocolate
2 tsp dark rum
2oz (50g) plain flour

TOPPING
1oz (25g) white
   chocolate, melted
1/2pt (300ml)
   whipped cream to
   serve

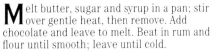

Melt butter, sugar and syrup in a pan; stir over gentle heat, then remove. Add chocolate and leave to melt. Beat in rum and flour until smooth; leave until cold.

Take a tsp of mixture and form into a smooth ball – repeat to make 20 balls.

Line 2 baking sheets with bakewell. Place 3 balls, spaced apart, on each baking sheet. Bake one sheet at a time in a preheated 375°F/190°C/Gas 5 oven for 4–5 minutes until mixture has stopped bubbling.

Have ready 3 thin-handled wooden spoons or oiled oranges; cool rum snaps for a few seconds, then lift off one at a time and wrap around handles to form tubes, or mould over oranges to make baskets. When set, slide off and cool. Repeat cooking and moulding snaps in batches as above.

Pipe zig-zag lines of white chocolate onto each tube and store in airtight containers until required. To serve, pipe cream into both ends of each rum snap.

CHOCOLATE SPRITZ COOKIES

Makes 60

4oz (100g) butter
4oz (100g) caster
   sugar
1 egg
7oz (200g) plain flour
½oz (15g) cocoa

TOPPINGS
chopped angelica,
   glacé cherries,
   hazelnuts and
   chocolate dots

Cream butter and sugar in a bowl until fluffy, then beat in egg. Sieve in flour and mix to a soft dough. Knead cocoa evenly into ½ dough.

Using a piping bag and ½″ (1cm) star nozzle or a biscuit machine, pipe ½ chocolate dough into stars onto baking sheets, and top with nuts.

Shape ½ plain dough into a roll, and match with a chocolate dough roll (using remaining cocoa dough). Place one on top of other in a piping bag or biscuit machine and pipe both doughs together to make various-shaped 2-tone cookies.

Pipe remaining plain dough into various shapes. Top each with angelica, cherries, nuts or dots.

Bake in a preheated 350°F/180°C/Gas 4 oven for 15 minutes. Loosen with a palette knife, cool, then store in an airtight jar.

FLORENTINES

Makes 15

2oz (50g) unsalted
butter
3oz (75g) caster sugar
3 tbsp single cream
2oz (50g) flaked
almonds
2oz (50g) candied peel
1oz (25g) skinned
hazelnuts, chopped
8 glacé cherries,
chopped
1½ tbsp plain flour

TOPPING
2oz (50g) plain eating
chocolate, melted
2oz (50g) white
chocolate, melted

Melt butter, sugar and cream in a pan, stir over a gentle heat, then remove. Stir in all remaining ingredients until well blended.

Line 3 baking sheets with bakewell, and drop 5 tsp of mixture, well spaced, on each.

Bake in a preheated 350°F/180°C/Gas 4 oven for 5–8 minutes until golden at edges. Leave to set on paper, then peel off carefully and cool.

Spread bases of half the florentines with plain chocolate and, using a fork, mark wavy lines. Repeat with white chocolate when thick on remaining florentines. When set, store in an airtight container.

OATIE NUT SQUARES

Makes 24

4oz (100g) butter
6oz (175g) light soft
  brown sugar
4oz (100g) golden
  syrup
4oz (100g) plain
  chocolate
2 eggs, beaten
4oz (100g) fine
  wholemeal self-
  raising flour
2oz (50g) medium
  oatmeal
4oz (100g) pecan nuts
  or walnuts, chopped

TOPPING
6oz (175g) plain eating
  chocolate, melted
sliced pecan nuts to
  decorate

Melt butter, sugar and syrup in a pan, stir over gentle heat, then remove. Add chocolate and leave to melt. Stir in eggs, flour, oatmeal and nuts until well mixed.

Line a deep 11x7" (28x17.5cm) oblong tin with bakewell, pour in mixture and level top. Bake in a preheated 300°F/160°C/Gas 2 oven for about 1¼ hours until browned and firm to touch.

Cool in tin then turn onto a wire rack. Remove paper. Spread top evenly with melted chocolate, top with nuts, and leave to set before marking into 24 squares.

PALMIER COOKIES

Makes 40

6oz (175g) butter
4oz (100g) caster
  sugar
2 eggs, beaten
1lb (450g) plain flour
2 tsp baking powder
1oz (25g) custard
  powder
1oz (25g) drinking
  chocolate

Cream butter and sugar in a bowl until fluffy, then beat in eggs. Place ½ mixture in another bowl. Sieve ½ flour, ½ baking powder and custard powder into one bowl. Mix together to form a soft dough. Sieve remaining ingredients into second bowl and mix to a soft chocolate dough.

Roll out and trim each dough to a 10x8" (25x20cm) oblong. Wet chocolate dough and cover with plain dough. Roll both long sides into centre to make a double roll, press together, wrap in cling film and chill for ½ hour.

Cut dough into 40 ¼" (5mm) slices and place apart on bakewell-lined baking sheets. Bake in a preheated 350°F/180°C/Gas 4 oven for 10–15 minutes. Cool on a wire rack.

SHORTIE CARAMEL TRIANGLES

Makes 30

6oz (175g) plain flour
2oz (50g) caster sugar
4oz (100g) unsalted
  butter
1 tsp finely grated
  orange zest

FILLING

14oz (400g) can
  condensed milk
4oz (100g) unsalted
  butter
2oz (50g) caster sugar
2oz (50g) golden syrup
1 tsp vanilla essence
2oz (50g) raisins

TOPPING

5oz (150g) plain eating
  chocolate, melted
1oz (25g) white
  chocolate, melted

Sieve flour and sugar into a bowl, rub in butter and zest until mixture begins to bind together, then knead into a soft dough.

Line the base of an 11x7″ (28x17.5cm) swiss roll tin with bakewell. Roll and trim shortbread to fit base. Prick with a fork and bake in a preheated 350°F/180°C/Gas 4 oven for 20 minutes. Cool.

Put all filling ingredients except raisins in a pan and stir over gentle heat until melted. Bring, stirring, slowly to boil, then boil until thick, golden brown and mixture holds a trail on surface when spoon is lifted.

Sprinkle raisins over shortbread, pour over caramel and spread evenly to cover.

When caramel is cold, spread plain chocolate over evenly. Pipe lines of white chocolate backwards and forwards over plain chocolate. When set, cut into 30 triangles.

STRIPY CIGARETTES

Makes 25

2 egg whites
3 1/2 oz (85g) caster
  sugar
2oz (50g) plain flour
2oz (50g) unsalted
  butter, melted
1 oz (25g) plain
  chocolate, melted

Whisk egg whites in a bowl until stiff and add sugar gradually, whisking well after each addition. Add flour and butter and whisk until smooth.

Line 2 baking sheets with bakewell. Drop 3x1 tsp mixture, spaced apart, on each. Spread into rounds. Pipe lines of chocolate over each round.

Bake one sheet at a time in a preheated 375°F/190°C/Gas 5 oven for 3–4 minutes until pale brown at edges. Loosen with a palette knife and return to oven for 1 minute.

Taking one hot round at a time, roll around a pencil or thin wooden spoon handle, or mould over oiled oranges to make baskets; remove when firm (a few seconds). Repeat baking and moulding in batches as above to make 25 cigarette biscuits.

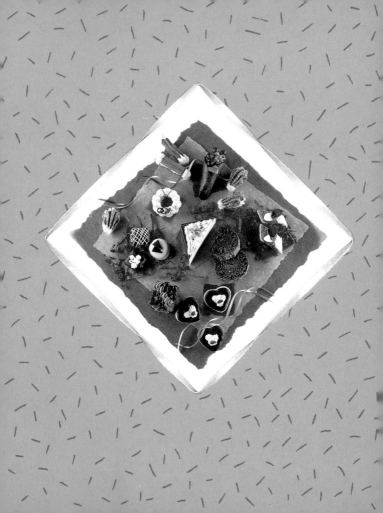

Fancy Cakes

Miniature assemblies of cakes, creamy fillings and fruit make mouthfuls of chocolate tea-time delights.

Tea-time is always popular despite the healthy eating movement and calorie counting. Invite a few friends or family to tea or coffee and serve a few fancy cakes for a real treat.

In this chapter are simple recipes for moist chocolate cake, which keeps well in a tin (if it lasts that long!), rich and sticky black bottom cakes with a surprise cream cheese centre, and Viennese fingers. For more indulgent cakes, try offering a selection of chocolate iced fancies, japonnaise shells or meringues. Light and dainty, they look pretty decorated with sugar flowers.

Many recipes included here could be served as an after-dinner dessert as well as for tea: berry cones, with any fruit in season of your choice, cherry triangles, redcurrant squares and minstrel gâteaux.

Make the meringues, the cake bases, cones and rings, and the japonnaise shells in advance and assemble them when they are required.

CHOCOLATE REDCURRANT CONES

Makes 15

BISCUIT MIXTURE
2oz (50g) icing sugar
1½oz (40g) plain flour
½oz (15g) cocoa
1 egg, separated
2 tbsp vegetable oil
3 tbsp milk

FILLING AND TOPPING
2oz (50g) plain chocolate, melted
½pt (300ml) cream, whipped
8oz (225g) redcurrants

Sieve icing sugar, flour and cocoa into a bowl. Add egg yolk, oil and milk; beat until smooth. Stiffly beat egg white and fold into chocolate mixture.

Line 3 baking sheets with bakewell. Mark 5 3½" (8.5cm) circles on each, and invert paper. Divide mixture between circles, spreading thinly to edges.

Bake, one sheet at a time, in a preheated 350°F/180°C/Gas 4 oven for 3–4 minutes. Loosen one round at a time and wrap around an oiled horn tin; remove when set (a few seconds). Repeat baking and moulding as above in batches to make 15 cones.

Stir melted chocolate into cream evenly. Fill each cone with cream and redcurrants.

BLACK BOTTOM CAKES

Makes 24

FILLING
8oz (225g) cream
  cheese
1oz (25g) caster sugar
1 egg
3oz (75g) chocolate
  dots

CAKE
10oz (300g) self-
raising flour

1oz (25g) cocoa
1½ tsp baking powder
8oz (225g) caster
  sugar
½pt (300ml) water
4floz (100ml)
  vegetable oil
1½ tbsp vinegar
1½ tsp vanilla essence
icing sugar to dust

Beat cream cheese, sugar and egg in a
bowl until fluffy, then stir in chocolate
dots evenly.

Sieve flour, cocoa and baking powder in a
bowl; stir in sugar. Whisk together water, oil,
vinegar and vanilla essence, then stir into
dry ingredients and beat until smooth.

Place 24 paper cake cases into bun trays.
Fill with chocolate mixture, then drop 1 tsp
cream cheese mixture into each. Bake in a
preheated 350°F/180°C/Gas 4 oven for 25–30
minutes until firm to touch. Cool on a wire
rack and sift with icing sugar.

CHOCOLATE CHERRY TRIANGLES

Makes 24

4-egg genoese sponge
(p.56)
4 tbsp morello cherry
jam
6oz (175g) white
chocolate, melted
8oz (225g) plain
chocolate, melted
½pt (300ml) cream,
whipped
8oz (225g) sugar-
frosted flowers
(p.153) to decorate

Make a 13x9" (32.5x23cm) sponge (p.56).
Cut cake into 24 2" (5cm) squares and
cut each square diagonally in half. Sandwich
pairs of triangles together with jam.

Make 24 2" (5cm) squares white
chocolate and 48 1½x2" (4x5cm) oblongs
plain chocolate (see cut-outs, p.149).

Spread sides of each cake with some
cream. Press a white chocolate piece onto
long side of each cake and two plain
chocolate pieces onto short sides. Pipe
cream over and top with sugar-frosted
flowers.

CHOCOLATE MERINGUE GARLANDS

Makes 20

MERINGUE
2 egg whites
4oz (100g) caster
sugar
2oz (50g) grated plain
chocolate

FILLING
½pt (300ml) cream,
whipped
40 piped chocolate
pieces (p.154) to
decorate

Whisk egg whites until stiff and gradually add caster sugar, whisking well after each addition until meringue stands up in peaks. Fold in grated chocolate and place in a large piping bag with a small star nozzle.

Line 2 baking sheets with bakewell. Draw 20 2½" (6cm) circles on each, and invert paper. Pipe stars of meringue around each circle and bake in a preheated oven at lowest setting for 1½ hours until crisp and dry. Cool.

Sandwich pairs of meringues together with cream. Pipe a small cream star on each. Decorate with chocolate pieces.

CHOCOLATE MERINGUE HEARTS

Makes 20

MERINGUE
2 egg whites
4¹/₂oz (115g) icing
  sugar, sieved
1oz (25g) plain
  chocolate, melted

**FILLING AND
TOPPING**
3oz (75g) plain
  confectioner's
  chocolate, melted
¹/₂pt (300ml) cream,
  whipped
sugar-frosted violet
  petals (p.153) to
  decorate

Line 2 baking sheets with bakewell. Draw 20 hearts on each piece of paper (using a 1¹/₂" (4cm) heart-shaped cutter as a guide) and invert paper.

Whisk egg whites and icing sugar in a bowl over a pan of hot water until thick. Whisk until mixture is cool and leaves a trail on surface. Fold in chocolate evenly. Place in a large piping bag fitted with a ¹/₄" (5mm) plain nozzle.

Pipe around outline of each heart with meringue. Fill in centres of only 20. Bake in a preheated oven at lowest setting for 1¹/₂ hours until crisp and dry. Cool.

Dip top of each heart frame into chocolate and leave to set on bakewell. Pipe swirls of cream on remaining hearts and top with a chocolate coated heart and sugared petals.

ICED CHOCOLATE FANCIES

Makes 15

GENOESE SPONGE
4 eggs
4oz (100g) caster
 sugar
3½oz (90g) plain flour
½oz (15g) cocoa
2oz (50g) unsalted
 butter, melted

TOPPINGS
4oz (100g) milk
 chocolate
4oz (100g) plain
 chocolate
4floz (100ml) milk
2 tbsp apricot jam,
 warmed
4oz (100g) white
 chocolate, melted
piped chocolate pieces
 (p.154), curls (p.144)
 and cut-outs (p.149)
 to decorate

Whisk eggs and sugar together in a bowl over a pan of hot water until thick. Remove bowl and whisk until mixture is thick and holds a trail on surface.

Sieve flour and cocoa and fold into mixture with melted butter until smooth. Pour into a bakewell-lined 13x9" (32.5x 23cm) swiss roll tin.

Bake in a preheated 350°F/180°C/Gas 4 oven for 15–20 minutes until firm to touch. Turn out, remove paper and cool.

Melt milk and plain chocolate each with

2floz (50ml) milk in separate pans until smooth. Cool until thick.

Cut sponge cake into 10 2″ (5cm) squares, 12 triangles and 8 rounds (using a 2″ (5cm) plain cutter). Sandwich matching-shaped cakes together with jam and place on a wire rack. Coat round cakes with white chocolate, and triangle and square cakes with milk and plain chocolate. Leave to set. Decorate cakes with piped chocolate, curls and cut-outs.

JAPONNAISE SHELLS

Makes 20

JAPONNAISE
2oz (50g) ground almonds
½oz (15g) cornflour
½oz (15g) cocoa
3oz (75g) caster sugar
2 egg whites

FILLING AND TOPPING
½pt (300ml) cream, whipped
2oz (50g) white chocolate, melted

Mix almonds, cornflour, cocoa and ½ sugar together in a bowl. Whisk egg whites until stiff. Add remaining sugar, whisking until mixture peaks. Carefully fold in almond mixture and place in a piping bag fitted with a medium star nozzle.

Line 2 baking sheets with bakewell, and pipe 20 shells onto each. Bake in a preheated 325°F/170°C/Gas 3 oven for 30–35 minutes. Cool on paper.

Sandwich pairs of japonnaise shells together with cream. Dip tapered end of each into melted chocolate. Leave on paper to set.

LITTLE CHOCOLATE TRUFFLE ROLLS

Makes 12

CAKE
3 eggs
1½oz (40g) caster
    sugar
1oz (25g) plain flour
3 tsp cocoa

FILLING
2oz (50g) plain
    chocolate, melted
¼pt (150ml) cream,
    whipped
12 chocolate rose
    leaves (p.148) to
    decorate

Line a 12″ (30cm) baking tray with
bakewell. Whisk eggs and sugar in a bowl
until thick and mixture holds a trail.

Divide mixture in half. Sieve ¾ flour over
one half and remaining flour and cocoa over
other. Fold in carefully.

Using a piping bag fitted with a ½″
(1cm) plain nozzle, pipe lines of plain
mixture over length of baking sheet, spaced
evenly apart. Fill in with lines of chocolate
mixture.

Bake in a preheated 400°F/200°C/Gas 6
oven for 5–8 minutes. Turn out, and peel off
paper when cool. Trim edges and cut in half
across stripes. Turn pieces over.

Fold chocolate into cream and spread
over each half of sponge. Roll up each into a
long thin roll (so stripes go across roll), wrap
in cling film and chill until firm. Cut into 12
diagonal rolls and decorate with chocolate
rose leaves, secured with chocolate cream.

REDCURRANT CHOCOLATE SQUARES

Makes 12

CAKE
4 eggs
4oz (100g) caster
  sugar
2 tbsp boiling water
6oz (175g) plain
  chocolate, melted
1oz (25g) plain flour

FILLING AND
  TOPPING
6floz (175ml) double
  cream
2oz (50g) plain
  chocolate, melted
12oz (350g)
  redcurrants
2 tbsp redcurrant jelly,
  melted

Whisk eggs and sugar together in a bowl until thick and leaves a trail. Stir in water and chocolate until well blended. Sieve flour and fold in carefully.

Pour mixture into a bakewell-lined 13x9" (32.5x23cm) swiss roll tin. Bake in a preheated 375°F/190°C/Gas 5 oven for 20–25 minutes.

Cool in tin, covered with a damp tea towel. Turn out, remove paper and cut cake in half across width.

Whip cream and chocolate together until thick. Spread ⅔ in a layer over one half cake and top with ⅔ redcurrants. Place other cake half on top. Brush with redcurrant jelly.

Cut cake into 12x2" (5cm) squares. Pipe remaining cream on top and decorate with remaining redcurrants. Brush fruit with jelly.

TIPSY FRUIT RINGS

Makes 8

CAKE
3 tsp cocoa
1 tbsp boiling water
2oz (50g) self-raising
  flour
1/2 tsp baking powder
2oz (50g) caster sugar
2oz (50g) soft
  margarine
1 egg

SYRUP AND
  FILLING
5oz (150g) caster sugar
6floz (175ml) water
2 tbsp tia maria
8oz (225g) mixed
  seasonal fruits, sliced

Blend cocoa and water together in a bowl until smooth. Cool. Place all remaining cake ingredients into a bowl, mix together, then beat until smooth.

Lightly grease 8 4½" (12cm) ring moulds. Divide mixture between moulds and bake in a preheated 325°F/170°C/Gas 3 oven for 20 minutes until firm to touch. Turn out of moulds and cool.

Dissolve sugar in water in a pan over gentle heat, and boil rapidly until syrupy. Cool slightly and stir in tia maria.

Divide syrup between moulds, replace sponge rings and leave to soak for a few minutes. Just before serving, turn out and fill centres with fruit.

VIENNESE FINGERS

Makes 20

8oz (225g) unsalted
butter
2oz (50g) icing sugar
7½oz (215g) plain
flour
½oz (15g) cocoa

FILLING AND
TOPPING

1½oz (40g) unsalted
butter
3oz (75g) icing sugar,
sieved
2 tsp lemon juice
3oz (75g) white
chocolate, melted

Cream butter and icing sugar in a bowl
until fluffy. Sieve in flour and cocoa, and
stir to form a soft dough.

Place dough in a piping bag fitted with a
medium star nozzle. Line 2 baking sheets
with bakewell. Pipe 20 3″ (7.5cm) lengths of
mixture onto each baking sheet.

Bake in a preheated 325°F/170°C/Gas 3
oven for 20–25 minutes. Cool.

Beat butter, icing sugar and lemon juice
in a bowl until fluffy. Sandwich pairs of
fingers together with icing and dip both ends
of each into melted chocolate. Leave to set.

SWISS CHOCOLATE LOG

Makes 16

CHOCOLATE SWISS ROLL

3 eggs
3oz (75g) caster sugar
2¹/₂oz (65g) self-raising
   flour
¹/₂oz (15g) cocoa
caster sugar to sprinkle

RICH CHOCOLATE CREAM

3oz (75g) caster sugar
5 tbsp water
3 egg yolks
6oz (175g) unsalted
   butter
3oz (75g) plain
   chocolate, melted
icing sugar to dust

Whisk eggs and sugar in a bowl over a pan of hot water until thick, then remove bowl. Whisk until mixture holds a trail. Sieve in flour and cocoa; fold in carefully.

Pour mixture into a bakewell-lined 13x9″ (32.5x23cm) swiss roll tin. Bake in a preheated 375°F/190°C/Gas 5 oven for 15–18 minutes until firm to the touch. Invert onto sugared bakewell, trim edges and roll up from the short end with paper inside. Cool.

Dissolve sugar and water in a pan, stirring over gentle heat. Boil rapidly until syrupy. (To test thread stage: press a drop between 2 teaspoons; when pulled apart, a thread will form between the spoons.) Gradually pour onto egg yolks in a bowl, whisking until thick. Beat butter until fluffy, and gradually beat in egg mixture until thick and fluffy. Fold in cooled chocolate.

Unroll swiss roll, remove paper, spread with ⅓ chocolate cream and re-roll. Spread outside of roll with remaining cream; mark lines with a fork. Chill for ½ hour. Sift with icing sugar and cut into ½″ (1cm) slices.

MINSTREL GÂTEAU

Serves 12

CAKE
3oz (75g) self-raising
  flour
1oz (25g) cocoa
4oz (100g) caster
  sugar
4 eggs, separated
2 tbsp vegetable oil
3 tbsp boiling water

TOPPING
6oz (175g) plain
  chocolate
1/2pt (300ml) milk
1/4pt (150ml) cream,
  whipped
8oz (225g) red- and
  blackcurrants

Sieve flour and cocoa into a bowl, stir in sugar, egg yolks, oil and water and beat until smooth. Whisk egg whites stiffly, and fold into cake mixture until evenly mixed.

Pour mixture into a base-lined 8" (20cm) cake tin. Bake in a preheated 350°F/180°C/Gas 4 oven for 45–50 minutes until firm to touch. Turn out and cool.

Melt chocolate and milk in a pan, stirring over gentle heat. Bring to boil, then cool until thick.

Split cake into 3 layers. Cover 2 layers with cream and currants (1/3 on each layer). Sandwich layers together and place third cake layer on top.

Cover cake with chocolate icing and leave to set. Pipe top with remaining cream and decorate with currants. Slice to serve.

MOIST CHOCOLATE CAKE

Makes 16

CAKE
6 tbsp golden syrup
2 tbsp black treacle
7 tbsp vegetable oil
4oz (100g) light soft
  brown sugar
1/4pt (150ml) milk
7oz (200g) plain flour
1oz (25g) cocoa
1/2 tsp bicarbonate of
  soda
1 egg

TOPPING
4oz (100g) plain
  chocolate, melted
1oz (25g) white
  chocolate, melted

Place syrup, treacle, oil, sugar and milk in a saucepan; stir over gentle heat until sugar has dissolved.

Sieve flour, cocoa and bicarbonate of soda into a bowl; add egg and syrup mixture and beat until smooth.

Pour into a 7" (17.5cm) square bakewell-lined tin and bake in a preheated 300°F/150°C/Gas 2 oven for 1–1¼ hours until firm when pressed in centre. Cool.

Spread top of cake with plain chocolate. Pipe on lines of white chocolate and draw a cocktail stick through the lines to make a pattern. Cut into 1½" (4cm) squares to serve.

Pastries

Light and flaky, sweet and short,
puffed up like pillows or paper thin,
here are pastry treats full of
chocolate temptations.

Pastry is a useful medium, being a carriage for all sorts of flavours and textures. It also lends itself to any shape, producing here a variety of irresistible chocolate recipes.

Choux pastry always sounds difficult, but really is straightforward to make. It can be spooned or piped into different shapes and when baked is like pillows of puffed-up pastry. Fill with fruit or chocolate cream to make special desserts or tea-time treats.

Filo pastry, available frozen, can be used leaf by leaf to enclose fruits and chocolate fillings in paper-thin layers; quick and easy to make but always special and unusual.

Sweet and shortcrust pastry will transform custards into tarts or boats, and fruit into tartlets or flans; if you do not have the exact size of tins given on the recipe, bun tins are perfectly acceptable.

Puff pastry, home or pre-made, is crisp, light and rich; leftover strips can be turned into chocolate twists or palmiers.

CHOCOLATE CANNOLI

Makes 16

PASTRY
4½oz (115g) plain
  flour
½oz (15g) cocoa
1oz (25g) butter
1 tsp caster sugar
4 tbsp sherry
oil for frying

FILLING
8oz (225g) ricotta
  cheese
4 tbsp sour cream
4oz (100g) glacé fruits,
  chopped
icing sugar to dust

Sieve flour and cocoa into a bowl; rub in butter finely. Stir in sugar and sherry, and mix to a soft dough. Wrap in cling film and chill.

Roll out pastry very thinly. Using a 4" (10cm) plain cutter, cut out 16 rounds. Heat oil in a deep pan to 375°F/190°C.

Wrap each pastry circle one at a time around an oiled wooden dowel or metal tube, 1" (2.5cm) diameter and 5" (12cm) long. Fry for 2 minutes until crisp; slide off mould and drain on kitchen paper. Repeat to make 16.

Mix all filling ingredients together. Pipe into each end of chocolate cannoli and dust with icing sugar.

CHOCOLATE AND APPLE STRUDEL

Makes 18

FILLING
2oz (50g) ground almonds
2oz (50g) plain chocolate, grated
2 dessert apples, peeled and grated
4oz (100g) fromage frais

PASTRY
9 sheets filo pastry, thawed
3oz (75g) butter, melted
icing sugar to dust

Mix all filling ingredients together in a bowl. Cut filo pastry sheets in half across width, place in a stack and cover to prevent drying.

Brush a piece of filo with melted butter and place a spoonful of filling at top edge. Fold side edges inwards, brush with more butter and roll up neatly. Repeat to make 18 rolls.

Place on baking sheet, brush with remaining butter and bake in a preheated 375°F/190°C/Gas 5 oven for 15 minutes. Cool and dredge with icing sugar.

CHOCOLATE CINNAMON MERINGUE BOATS

Makes 12

SWEET PASTRY
4oz (100g) plain flour
2 tsp icing sugar
3oz (75g) unsalted
  butter
1 egg yolk

FILLING
1oz (25g) plain
  chocolate
1/4pt (150ml) milk
1/2oz (15g) butter
2 eggs, separated
1 tsp cornflour
1/2 tsp ground cinnamon
2oz (50g) caster sugar

Sieve flour and icing sugar into a bowl. Rub butter in finely, add egg yolk and mix to a soft dough. Roll out and line 12 greased barquette moulds. Chill.

Stir chocolate, milk and butter in a pan over gentle heat. Bring to boil. Blend egg yolks, cornflour and cinnamon together in a bowl. Stir in milk and return mixture to pan; bring to boil, stirring. Cool.

Fill pastry boats with chocolate filling and bake in a preheated 375°F/190°C/Gas 5 oven for 10 minutes until filling has set.

Meanwhile, whisk egg whites stiffly. Whisk in sugar until thick. Pipe meringue on top of each boat and return to a 300°F/150°C/Gas 2 oven for 20 minutes until lightly browned. Cool.

CHOCOLATE REDCURRANT RINGS

Makes 10

2-egg quantity choux
   pastry (p.82)
2 tsp cocoa

FILLING
¹/₄pt (150ml) Greek
   yogurt
2 tsp caster sugar

¹/₄pt (150ml) double
   cream, whipped
12oz (350g)
   redcurrants
4 tbsp redcurrant jelly,
   melted
1oz (25g) flaked
   almonds, toasted, to
   decorate
icing sugar to dust

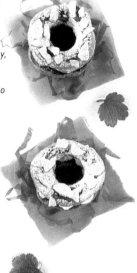

Make pastry (see p.82–83), replacing 2
tsp of flour with cocoa.

Pipe mixture into 10 rings on 2 greased
baking sheets (5 on each) and bake in a
preheated 400°F/200°C/Gas 6 oven for
25–30 minutes. Split rings and cool.

Fold yogurt and sugar into cream until
evenly blended. Mix together redcurrants
and jelly. Fill base of each ring with
redcurrant mixture. Pipe in yogurt cream
and replace tops. Brush with jelly.

Sprinkle with almonds and dust with
icing sugar.

CHOCOLATE FUDGE SLICE

Makes 14

PASTRY
6oz (175g) plain flour
3oz (75g) butter
cold water to mix

FILLING
1oz (25g) butter
2oz (50g) plain
 chocolate, melted

3oz (75g) light soft
 brown sugar
6oz (175g) caster
 sugar
3floz (75ml) milk
2oz (50g) golden
 syrup
1 tsp vanilla essence
3 eggs
4oz (100g) pecan nuts
icing sugar to dust

Place flour in a bowl and rub in butter finely. Mix to soft dough with water. Roll out to line a 14x4¼" (35x11cm) fluted flan tin. Prick with a fork and chill.

Bake blind in a preheated 400°F/200°C/ Gas 6 oven for 10 minutes. Remove and reduce oven to 325°F/170°C/Gas 3.

Add butter to chocolate and stir until melted. Stir in all remaining filling ingredients and beat until smooth.

Pour into pastry case and return to oven for 35–40 minutes until filling has set and is golden brown. Cool in tin before dusting with icing sugar. Cut into 1" (2.5cm) slices.

CHOCOLATE FRUIT TARTS

Makes 10

4oz (100g) sweet
pastry (p.73)

FILLING

4oz (100g) plain
chocolate, melted
2 tbsp ready-made
custard
1 tbsp marsala
1/4pt (150ml) double
cream, whipped
1lb (450g) mixed fresh
fruit: raspberries,
grapes, strawberries,
red- and
blackcurrants
4 tbsp redcurrant jelly,
melted

Make pastry (p.73). Roll out thinly and
line 10 individual brioche tins. Prick
bases with a fork and chill.

Bake blind in a preheated 400°F/200°C/
Gas 6 oven for 10–15 minutes. Cool. Brush
inside of tarts with melted chocolate. Leave
to set.

Fold custard and marsala into cream.
Divide evenly between tart cases.

Fill with fruit and glaze with redcurrant
jelly. Leave to set.

CHOCOLATE CUSTARD TARTS

Makes 12

4oz (100g) sweet
   pastry (p.73)

FILLING
8floz (225ml) milk
2oz (50g) plain
   chocolate
2 eggs, beaten
white chocolate curls
   (p.144) to decorate

Make pastry (p.73). Roll out thinly and cut out 12 3½" (8.5cm) rounds. Use to line a bun tin tray and chill.

Heat milk and chocolate in a pan over gentle heat. Stir until melted. Pour onto beaten eggs, stirring. Strain into a jug.

Fill each pastry case with custard and bake in a preheated 375°F/190°C/Gas 5 oven for 5 minutes, then reduce oven to 325°F/170°C/Gas 3 for 10–15 minutes until custard has set. Cool in tin before turning out. Decorate with chocolate curls.

CHOCOLATE KNOTS

Makes 20

4½oz (115g) plain
   flour
½oz (15g) cocoa
½ tsp baking powder
1oz (25g) butter
2 tbsp caster sugar
1 egg, beaten
oil for deep-frying
2 tsp icing sugar
½ tsp ground cinnamon

Sieve flour, cocoa and baking powder into a bowl. Rub in butter finely, then stir in sugar and egg and mix to a soft dough. Wrap in cling film and chill.

Heat oil in a deep-fat pan to 375°F/190°C.

Divide dough into 20 pieces. Roll out each piece thinly and tie into a knot. Fry pastry knots in 3 batches until well risen and evenly coloured. Drain on kitchen paper.

Mix icing sugar and cinnamon together and sift over chocolate knots. Serve hot.

CHOCOLATE PALMIERS

Makes 10 or 20

PASTRY
1 tbsp icing sugar
8oz (225g) puff pastry,
   thawed

FILLING
2 tbsp double cream
2oz (50g) plain
   chocolate, grated
whipped cream to serve
   (optional)

Sprinkle work surface with icing sugar. Roll out pastry and trim to a 12" (30cm) square. Cut in half, then spread both halves with cream and sprinkle with chocolate.

Roll 2 short edges of each half into centre. Press together firmly. Cover with cling film, and chill until firm.

Cut each half into 10 slices and arrange on a bakewell-lined baking sheet. Bake in a preheated 425°F/220°C/Gas 7 oven for 8–10 minutes. Cool and serve separately or in pairs filled with whipped cream.

CHOCOLATE TWISTS

Makes 30

*8oz (225g) puff pastry,
    thawed
1 tbsp chocolate spread
icing sugar to dust*

Roll out and trim pastry to an oblong 18x9" (46x23cm). Cut in half across the width.

Warm chocolate spread until liquid, then brush evenly over one pastry half. Place other half on top.

Cut into 30 strips. Twist each strip and arrange on a bakewell-lined baking sheet. Chill. Bake in a preheated 425°F/220°C/Gas 7 oven for 8–10 minutes. Cool before dusting with icing sugar.

WHITE AND DARK CHOCOLATE PUFFS

Makes 30

CHOUX PASTRY
4½floz (115ml) water
2oz (50g) butter
2½oz (65g) plain flour
2 eggs

FILLING
¼pt (150ml) milk
1 egg yolk
½oz (15g) plain flour
½oz (15g) caster sugar
½ tsp vanilla essence
¼pt (150ml) double
    cream, whipped

TOPPING
2oz (50g) white
    chocolate, melted
1½floz (40ml) milk
2oz (50g) plain
    chocolate, melted

Heat water and butter in a pan until melted. Bring to boil, then beat in flour to form a ball of dough. Beat in eggs gradually and thoroughly.

Pipe 30 balls of mixture onto a baking sheet. Bake in a preheated 400°F/200°C/Gas 6 oven for 20–25 minutes. Slit each bun and cool on a wire rack.

Blend a little milk with egg yolk, flour, sugar and vanilla in a bowl. Bring remainder to boil in a pan. Pour onto egg mixture, stirring, then return to pan. Bring to boil, stirring. Cook for 2 minutes. Cover surface with cling film and leave until cold. Fold in cream.

Pipe filling into choux buns. Dip 8 into white chocolate. Stir milk into plain chocolate and dip remaining buns. Leave to set.

FLAKY APRICOT PASTRIES

Makes 10

10 apricots, halved and
   stones removed
5 sheets filo pastry,
   thawed
2oz (50g) butter,
   melted
1 egg white, beaten
caster sugar to sprinkle

FILLING
8floz (225ml) milk
1oz (25g) plain
   chocolate
2oz (50g) ground rice
¼ tsp ground nutmeg
1 tsp caster sugar

First make filling: heat milk and chocolate
in a pan over gentle heat and stir until
melted. Bring to boil, sprinkle in rice,
nutmeg and sugar; stir until mixture
thickens, then cook for 3 minutes. Cool.

Fill centre of each apricot with rice
filling and press halves together. Cut filo
pastry into 30 squares, brush both sides with
melted butter, place in a stack and cover.

Take 3 squares of pastry at a time and
place an apricot in centre. Draw up edges to
enclose apricot and twist to seal. Repeat to
make 10 in all.

Brush with egg white and sprinkle with
sugar. Arrange on a bakewell-lined baking
sheet and bake in a preheated 375°F/190°C/
Gas 5 oven for 15–20 minutes. Cool.

FLAKY CHOCOLATE FINGERS

Makes 16

PASTRY
8oz (225g) puff pastry,
   thawed

FILLING
4oz (100g) cream
   cheese

2 tbsp natural yogurt
2oz (50g) plain
   chocolate, melted
8oz (225g) raspberries
2oz (50g) white
   chocolate, melted
plain chocolate curls
   (p.144) to decorate

Cut pastry into 3 and roll out each piece to an oblong 10x4" (25x10cm). Place each strip on a wetted baking sheet. Prick with a fork and chill for ½ hour.

Bake in a preheated 425°F/220°C/Gas 7 oven for 10–15 minutes until golden brown. Cool.

Beat cream cheese and yogurt together in a bowl until smooth. Stir in plain chocolate.

Trim pastry oblongs neatly so all same size. Spread 2 layers with chocolate filling and cover each with ⅓ raspberries; place one on top of other and top with plain layer.

Spread white chocolate evenly over top and chill to set. Decorate with remaining raspberries and chocolate curls. Cut into 1" (2.5cm) slices to serve.

Desserts

*Dreamy desserts for summer days
and warming winter puddings to
look forward to on a chilly day; all
on a chocolate theme.*

Chocolate desserts are always a favourite – although people may not admit to eating or enjoying them, when a tempting display is put on the table it is amazing how quickly they all disappear.

This chapter contains dreamy desserts suitable for entertaining and special occasions to more homely puddings.

For family desserts, try Oliver's chocolate pudding, which is a light sponge that floats on a rich chocolate sauce: it is a favourite in our home and is aptly named as everyone, without exception, asks for more! The chocolate soufflé puddings are light but warming, and the raspberry chocolate mallow is always a great choice for children.

When entertaining, serve the three chocolates with lime sauce – a blend of three chocolates, subtly flavoured and complemented with the sweet scent of lime; served in tiny dishes, they look delectably pretty. Or, for a romantic dinner for two, serve the coeur à la chocolate crème – heart-shaped mouthfuls of smooth chocolate cream accompanied by fresh fruits of the season.

CHOCOLATE CHEESE FRUIT CUPS

Makes 10

CHOCOLATE CUPS

2oz (50g) white
  chocolate, melted
6oz (175g) plain or
  milk eating
  chocolate, melted

FILLING

8oz (225g) cream
  cheese
4 tbsp Greek yogurt
2 tsp sugar
1 ogen melon, cut into
  balls
8oz (225g) blueberries
  and redcurrants

Place 10 paper cake cases in a bun tray. Pipe zig-zag lines of white chocolate inside each case and chill until set. Carefully coat inside of each case with plain chocolate, making sure there are no gaps. Chill, then peel off paper.

Beat cream cheese, yogurt and sugar together in a bowl.

Divide ⅔ fruit between each chocolate cup, top with cream cheese filling and decorate with remaining fruit.

CHOCOLATE, PASSION AND LIME MOUSSE

Makes 6

8oz (225g) Greek yogurt
8oz (225g) white chocolate, melted

3 passion fruit, seeded
finely grated rind 1 lime
2 tsp lime juice
lime slices to decorate

Place yogurt in a bowl over hot water and gently warm; stir in white chocolate until smooth.

Add passion fruit, lime rind and juice, and stir until evenly blended. Pour into 6 small dishes. Chill until firm.

Decorate with twists of lime.

CHOCOLATE SOUFFLÉ PUDDINGS

Makes 6

2oz (50g) butter, softened
3oz (75g) caster sugar
2 eggs, separated

1½oz (40g) plain flour
1 tbsp cocoa
12floz (350ml) milk
icing sugar to dust

Beat butter, sugar and egg yolks together in a bowl until fluffy.

Sieve flour and cocoa into mixture and mix. Stiffly whisk egg whites and fold into mixture with milk.

Pour mixture into 6 individual buttered soufflé dishes. Bake in a preheated 350°F/180°C/Gas 4 oven for 10–15 minutes until risen and set. Dust with icing sugar.

CHOCOLATE STRAWBERRY LAYERS

Makes 10

*6oz (175g) white
   chocolate, melted
6oz (175g) plain
   chocolate, melted
½pt (300ml) double
   cream
3 tbsp Greek yogurt
12oz (350g)
   strawberries, sliced*

Make 10 white and 10 plain chocolate squares using a 1½″ (4cm) fluted square cutter. (Follow instructions for chocolate cut-outs, p.149.) Repeat to make another 20 squares using a 1¼″ (3.5cm) cutter.

Whip cream and yogurt together until thick. Pipe a white and plain chocolate square with cream, then cover with strawberry slices. Place one on other and top with two small white and plain chocolate squares. Repeat to make 10. Chill.

CHOCOLATE VELVET

Makes 6

3 egg yolks
1/2pt (300ml) milk
1 tsp finely grated lime
  rind

4oz (100g) white
  chocolate, melted
2oz (50g) plain
  chocolate, melted
8 tbsp fromage frais

Beat egg yolks in a bowl. Bring milk to boil in a pan and pour into yolks, stirring well. Return custard to pan; heat gently, stirring constantly until it thickens. Do not boil or custard will curdle.

Add 1/2 custard and all lime rind to white chocolate and stir until smooth. Stir remaining custard into plain chocolate. Cool.

Fold 1/2 fromage frais into each chocolate mixture. Fill 6 small glasses with alternate spoonfuls of each mixture. Chill until ready to serve.

COEUR À LA CHOCOLATE CRÈME

Makes 6

2pt (1ltr) milk
6oz (175g) plain chocolate
1½ tsp rennet
¼pt (150ml) double cream
6oz (175g) mixed soft fruit to decorate

Heat ¼pt (150ml) of milk and chocolate in a pan over gentle heat. Stir occasionally until melted. Remove from heat. Add remaining milk and ensure liquid is at blood heat.

Stir in rennet and leave to set for 1 hour. Pour set curd into a muslin-lined sieve over a bowl. Leave for 4 hours or overnight until thick. Remove muslin.

Sieve curd through a fine sieve into a clean bowl. Lightly whip cream and fold into curds. Pour mixture into 6 *coeur à la crème* moulds lined with muslin on a tray.

Leave overnight in fridge to drain, then turn out, remove muslin and decorate with fresh fruit.

LITTLE POTS OF CHOCOLATE

Makes 6

3 eggs, separated
6oz (175g) plain
  chocolate, melted
2 tbsp dark rum
white and dark
  chocolate leaves
  (p.148) to decorate

Stir egg yolks into chocolate until well blended, then gradually stir in rum.

Whisk egg whites until stiff; fold into chocolate mixture until evenly mixed.

Divide mixture between 6 small pots. Chill for 1 hour. Decorate with chocolate leaves.

LITTLE CHOCOLATE CHEESECAKES

Makes 8

BISCUIT BASE
4oz (100g) digestive
  biscuits, crushed
1½oz (40g) unsalted
  butter, melted

TOPPING
8oz (225g) cream
  cheese
¼pt (150ml) single
  cream
1 egg yolk
1 tbsp orange juice
4oz (100g) milk eating
  chocolate, melted
white chocolate curls
  (p.144) to decorate

Mix together crumbs and butter. Divide between 8 bakewell-lined muffin rings on a lined baking sheet. Press well down.

Beat cream cheese, cream, egg yolk and juice together in a bowl until smooth. Stir in chocolate until evenly blended. Divide mixture between muffin rings, level top and chill for several hours or overnight.

Remove cheesecakes from rings and paper, and decorate tops with white chocolate curls.

OLIVER'S CHOCOLATE PUDDINGS

Makes 6

SPONGE

3oz (75g) butter,
    softened
3oz (75g) light soft
    brown sugar
3oz (75g) fine
    wholemeal self-
    raising flour
1 tbsp cocoa
2 eggs

SAUCE

3 tsp cocoa
2 tsp coffee granules
1 tbsp sugar
1 tbsp cornflour
½pt (300ml) boiling
    water
1oz (25g) unsalted
    butter
icing sugar to dust

Place all sponge ingredients in a bowl. Beat together until smooth and glossy. Divide mixture between 6 4½″ (11cm) buttered dishes.

Mix cocoa, coffee, sugar and cornflour together in a jug. Add boiling water and butter and whisk until smooth.

Immediately pour sauce over each sponge and bake in a preheated 375°F/190°C/ Gas 5 oven for 10–15 minutes until sponges are well risen on top of sauce. Sift icing sugar over and serve immediately.

THREE CHOCOLATES WITH LIME SAUCE

Makes 6

2oz (50g) white
chocolate, melted
2oz (50g) plain
chocolate, melted
2oz (50g) milk
chocolate, melted
1 tsp finely grated lime
rind
2 tsp lime juice
1 tbsp dark rum or
brandy
2 tsp strong coffee

3 egg yolks
5oz (150g) unsalted
butter
1/4pt (150ml) cream,
whipped

SAUCE
finely grated rind and
juice 2 limes
2 tsp cornflour
2oz (50g) caster sugar
lime twists to decorate

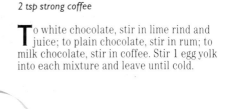

To white chocolate, stir in lime rind and
juice; to plain chocolate, stir in rum; to
milk chocolate, stir in coffee. Stir 1 egg yolk
into each mixture and leave until cold.

Beat butter until fluffy and light. Add ⅓ to each mixture and stir until blended. Fold ⅓ whipped cream into each mixture (do not over-mix).

Line 6 tiny moulds with cling film. Fill with alternate spoonful of each mixture. Chill for several hours or overnight.

Measure lime juice, and make up to 6floz (175ml) with water. Blend cornflour and sugar with juice in a pan; bring to boil and cook for 1 minute. Stir in lime rind and cool.

Turn out chocolate moulds and serve with lime sauce and decorate with tiny lime twists.

RASPBERRY CHOCOLATE MALLOWS

Makes 6

BASE
3oz (75g)
  marshmallows
1 tbsp orange juice
6oz (175g) petit beurre
  biscuits, crushed

TOPPING
2 eggs, separated
3oz (75g) plain
  chocolate, melted
2 tbsp sherry
12oz (350g)
  raspberries, sliced
whipped cream

Melt marshmallows and juice in a pan over gentle heat, stirring occasionally. Add biscuits; mix together well. Divide mixture between 6 dishes.

Stir egg yolks into chocolate with sherry. Cool. Whisk egg whites and fold into mixture.

Arrange a layer of raspberries over biscuit base, then top with chocolate mixture; leave until set, about ½ hour.

Decorate with piped cream and raspberries.

TINY CHOCOLATE CREAMS

Makes 6

4oz (100g) plain
  chocolate
1pt (550ml) milk
4 egg yolks
1oz (25g) caster sugar
¹/₂ tsp vanilla essence
¹/₂oz (15g) gelatine
3 tbsp boiling water
2 tbsp dark rum or
  orange juice
¹/₄pt (150ml) cream,
  whipped
sugar-frosted flowers
  (p.153) to decorate

Stir chocolate and milk in a pan over gentle heat until melted. Bring to boil.

Beat egg yolks, sugar and essence together in a bowl. Add milk, stirring. Rinse out pan, and return chocolate milk. Stir or whisk continuously over gentle heat until mixture thickens.

Dissolve gelatine in boiling water, then stir into chocolate with rum.

When mixture is beginning to set, fold in cream and pour into 6 individual moulds. Chill until firm. Turn out and decorate with sugared flowers.

TROPICAL PAVLOVAS

Makes 10

MERINGUE

3 egg whites
7oz (200g) caster
  sugar
2 tsp cocoa
1 tsp vinegar
1/2 tsp vanilla essence
2 tbsp chocolate dots

FILLING

6floz (175ml) double
  cream
4oz (100g) fromage
  frais
1 star fruit, sliced
1 ogen melon, scooped
  into balls
1/4 watermelon,
  scooped into balls

Whisk egg whites in a bowl until stiff; gradually whisk in sugar until thick.

Blend cocoa, vinegar and essence together and add to meringue, whisking until very thick and glossy.

Line a baking sheet with bakewell, mark on 10 3″ (7.5cm) circles and invert paper. Fill each circle with meringue, pipe a shell edging around each, and decorate with dots.

Bake in a preheated 275°F/140°C/Gas 2 oven for 45 minutes. Turn oven off and leave pavlovas in to cool. Remove when cold.

Whip cream until thick and fold in fromage frais. Mix fruit together, reserving 1/4 for decoration, and fold remainder into cream. Pile on filling and top with reserved fruit.

WHITE CHOCOLATE AND LEMON SOUFFLÉS

Makes 8

4 eggs, separated
2oz (50g) caster sugar
3oz (75g) white
    chocolate, melted
finely grated rind and
    juice 2 lemons
3 tsp gelatine
2 tbsp boiling water
½pt (300ml) cream,
    whipped
grated milk chocolate
    to decorate
lemon shreds to
    decorate

Around outside of 8 tiny soufflé dishes, secure bands of bakewell to stand 1" (2.5cm) above rims.

Whisk egg yolks and sugar over hot water until thick enough to hold a trail. Stir in chocolate, lemon rind and juice.

Dissolve gelatine in boiling water, stir into lemon mixture and leave until just beginning to set, stirring occasionally.

Whisk egg whites until almost stiff. Fold first cream and then egg whites carefully into lemon mixture until smooth. Divide between soufflé dishes, allowing mixture to come ½"(1cm) above rim. Chill until firm.

Remove paper. Press chocolate around outside and lemon shreds on top.

Ice Creams & Drinks

Cool, creamy creations to eat and
drink made from wonderful
combinations of white, milk and
plain chocolate.

Cool, creamy ice creams, tangy frozen sorbets, hot and frothy drinks, and cold chocolate fizzes are all included in this chapter.

The ice creams, with their own individual textures and flavours, are quick and easy to make. My daughters love the chocolate ripple ice cream, simply because they can make it by just mixing the ingredients together and freezing it. There are recipes for lime sorbet, served either in lime shells or little dishes, chocolate mint ice cream, a three-chocolate ice cream with each layer a different flavour and texture, and, smoothest of all, a rich chocolate ice cream. Serve them in tiny rum chocolate snaps, baskets, tuilles or stripy cigarette baskets (see biscuit section, p.47, for recipes).

Experiment with the drink recipes – they are simply a guide. Try, for instance, the lime fizz, banana frappé or pineapple cooler with a little added spirit to give them a zing. On a cold chilly night, warm yourself up with a hot rum toddie, or add brandy or rum to a cup of hot chocolate special for sipping in front of a blazing log fire.

CHOCOLATE RIPPLE ICE CREAM

Serves 8

14oz (400g) condensed
   milk
1pt (550ml) whipping
   cream, whipped
2 tbsp chocolate spread
chocolate cut-out
   hearts (p.149) to
   decorate

Fold condensed milk into cream carefully until evenly blended.

Warm chocolate spread until runny. Place ¼ cream mixture in a plastic container, and drizzle over ¼ chocolate spread. Swirl lightly with a skewer. Repeat, layering cream and chocolate spread.

Cover and freeze for several hours or overnight until firm. Serve in scoops, decorated with chocolate cut-outs.

CLEMENTINE, MANGO AND CHOCOLATE SORBET

Serves 6

6 clementines
1 mango, chopped
2oz (50g) caster sugar
2 tsp gelatine

2 tbsp boiling water
3oz (75g) white
    chocolate, melted
2 egg whites
fresh mint to decorate

Squeeze juice from clementines (reserve shells for serving if desired). Place with mango and sugar in a food processor. Blend together well.

Dissolve gelatine in boiling water. Stir into chocolate, and beat until smooth. Add to processor and blend until evenly mixed. Pour into a plastic container, cover and freeze for 1 hour or until partially frozen.

Scrape mixture into food processor again and blend until smooth. Stiffly beat egg whites, and fold into chocolate mixture. Return mixture to container and freeze for several hours or overnight until firm. Serve in clementine shells or small dishes, decorated with mint.

MINT CHIP ICE CREAM

Serves 12

3 tbsp cornflour
6oz (175g) caster
    sugar
1pt (550ml) milk
peppermint oil or
    essence
green food colouring
½pt (300ml) double
    cream, whipped
4oz (100g) plain or
    milk chocolate dots
large chocolate cut-out
    flowers (p.149) to
    serve (optional)
fresh mint to decorate

Blend together cornflour, sugar and milk in a pan. Bring to boil, stirring until thick, then cook over gentle heat for 2 minutes. Cover surface with cling film or bakewell and leave until cold.

Stir in a few drops of peppermint and food colouring to tint it pale green. Fold in cream until evenly blended.

Pour mixture into a plastic container, cover and freeze for about 2 hours or until partially frozen. Turn mixture into a bowl, break up and whisk until smooth. Fold in chocolate chips and return to plastic container.

Freeze for several hours or overnight until firm. Serve in scoops on large chocolate flowers if liked, and decorate with mint.

RICH CHOCOLATE ICE CREAM

Serves 6

¹/₄pt (150ml) single
  cream
3 egg yolks
2oz (50g) caster sugar
3oz (75g) plain
  chocolate
¹/₄pt (150ml) double
  cream, whipped
stripy cigarette baskets
  (p.47) to serve
  (optional)
white and plain
  chocolate leaves
  (p.148) to
  decorate

Beat cream, egg yolks and sugar together in a pan. Stir or whisk over gentle heat until thick – do not boil or it will curdle.

Add chocolate, allow to melt, then stir until evenly blended. Cover with cling film or bakewell and leave until cold.

Fold in cream and pour into a plastic container. Freeze for 2 hours until mixture is partially frozen.

Turn into a bowl, break up and whisk until smooth. Return to plastic container, cover and freeze for several hours or overnight until firm.

Serve scoops in stripy cigarette baskets, if liked, with chocolate leaves.

ORANGE AND CHOCOLATE FROMAGE FRAIS

Serves 8

1 lb (450g) fromage
    frais
finely grated rind and
    juice 1 orange
1 oz (25g) caster sugar
3 tsp gelatine
1 tbsp boiling water
1 tbsp hazelnut
    chocolate spread
4 chocolate rum snap
    baskets (p.40) to
    serve
orange shreds to
    decorate

Mix fromage frais, orange rind, juice and sugar together. Dissolve gelatine in boiling water, then stir into orange mixture.

Chill mixture until beginning to thicken, then whisk until smooth. Pour into a plastic container. Swirl hazelnut chocolate spread into mixture, then cover and freeze until it is firm.

Divide between 4 chocolate rum snap baskets and decorate with orange shreds to serve.

WHITE CHOCOLATE LIME SORBET

Serves 4—6

4 limes
¹/₄pt (150ml) water
2oz (50g) caster sugar
3oz (75g) white
  chocolate, melted
2 egg whites
lime rind to decorate

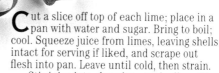

Cut a slice off top of each lime; place in a pan with water and sugar. Bring to boil; cool. Squeeze juice from limes, leaving shells intact for serving if liked, and scrape out flesh into pan. Leave until cold, then strain.

Stir juice into chocolate gradually until smooth. Pour into a plastic container and freeze for 1 hour or until partially frozen.

Scrape mixture into a bowl and whisk until smooth. Stiffly beat egg whites and whisk into mixture.

Fill each lime shell with sorbet, placing any spare in a container. Freeze for several hours until firm. Decorate with lime rind.

TRIO CHOCOLATE ICE CREAM

Serves 8

1pt (550ml) ready-
    made custard
3oz (75g) milk
    chocolate, melted
3oz (75g) plain
    chocolate, melted
3oz (75g) white
    chocolate, melted
1/2pt (300ml) double
    cream, whipped

Divide custard between 3 bowls. Stir milk chocolate into one bowl until evenly blended. Repeat with plain and white chocolates for remaining bowls of custard.

Divide cream between bowls, folding in until well mixed.

Freeze each ice cream separately in covered plastic containers for 2 hours or until partially set.

Turn each mixture into a bowl and whisk until smooth. Pour plain chocolate ice cream into base of a container, followed by white chocolate layer and then milk chocolate. Freeze for several hours or overnight until firm. Serve, cut into fancy slices.

CHOCOLATE BANANA FRAPPÉ

Serves 4

1oz (25g) white
   chocolate
1/2pt (300ml) milk
1 banana, peeled
4 scoops vanilla ice
   cream
cocoa to decorate
soda water
chocolate curls (p.144)
   to decorate

Stir chocolate and milk in a pan over
gentle heat until melted. Chill.

Place banana, ice cream and chocolate
mixture into a liquidizer; blend until smooth.

Just before serving, dip rims of 4 tall
glasses in cocoa. Divide mixture between
glasses, fill each with soda water and
decorate with chocolate curls.

CHOCOLATE LIME FIZZ

Serves 4

2oz (50g) white
  chocolate
¼pt (150ml) milk
finely grated rind and
  juice 2 limes

egg white and coloured
  sugar to frost
soda water
lime twists to decorate

Stir chocolate and milk in a pan over gentle heat until melted. Cool, stir in lime rind and juice and chill. Frost rims of 4 tall glasses by dipping into egg white and coloured sugar.

Just before serving, divide lime mixture between glasses and fill with soda water. Decorate with lime twists.

CHOCOLATE MILK SHAKE

Serves 4

2oz (50g) plain
  chocolate
1pt (550ml) milk
4 scoops vanilla ice
  cream

grated chocolate to
  sprinkle

Heat chocolate and 4 tbsp milk in a pan, stirring occasionally until melted. Take off heat. Chill.

Place with ½ ice cream and remaining milk in a liquidizer and blend until frothy. Pour into 4 tall glasses, add a scoop of ice cream to each and sprinkle with chocolate.

HONEYED RUM TODDIE

Serves 4

1½ tbsp cocoa
1pt (550ml) milk
1 egg
1 tbsp clear honey
2 tbsp dark rum or
   brandy
extra cocoa to sprinkle

H eat cocoa and milk in a pan and stir over
gentle heat. Bring to boil.
   Whisk in egg, honey and rum, and pour
into 4 heatproof glasses. Sprinkle with cocoa.

HOT CHOCOLATE SPECIAL

Serves 4

2oz (50g) plain
  chocolate
1pt (550ml) milk
4 tbsp whipped cream
cocoa to sprinkle

Heat chocolate and milk in a pan over gentle heat and stir until melted. Bring to boil. Pour into 4 heatproof glasses. Pipe or spoon cream on top and sprinkle with cocoa.

MOCHA CLOUD

Serves 4

2 tbsp drinking
  chocolate
2 tsp instant coffee
  powder

1 pt (550ml) milk
1 egg, separated
1 tbsp caster sugar

Heat drinking chocolate, 1½ tsp coffee and 4 tbsp milk in a pan, stirring until dissolved. Stir in egg yolk and chill.

Just before serving: stiffly whisk egg white and whisk in sugar.

Whisk remaining milk into mocha mixture. Pour into 4 glasses, top each with a spoonful of meringue and sprinkle with remaining coffee.

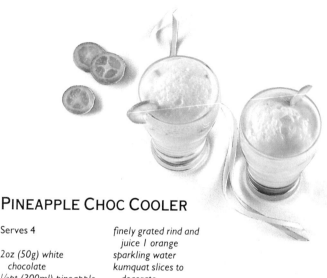

PINEAPPLE CHOC COOLER

Serves 4

2oz (50g) white
  chocolate
1/2pt (300ml) pineapple
  juice

finely grated rind and
  juice 1 orange
sparkling water
kumquat slices to
  decorate

Stir chocolate and 4 tbsp pineapple juice
in a pan over gentle heat until melted.
Add remaining juices and orange rind. Chill.
    Divide mixture between 4 tall glasses.
Fill each with sparkling water and decorate
with kumquat slices.

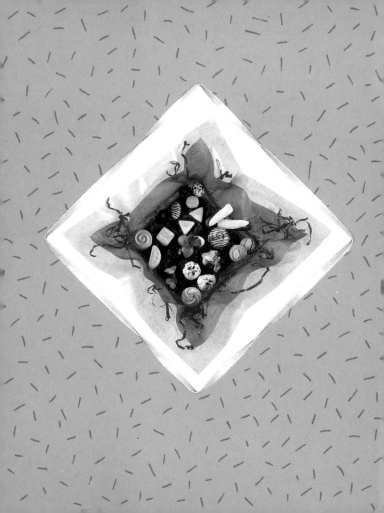

Chocolates & Sweets

*Sweet mouthfuls of tantalising
chocolate confections; rich, smooth
and in a myriad of flavours.*

No chocolate book would be complete without a chocolate and sweet section. These miniature confections are quite time-consuming but rewarding.

Hand-made chocolates packed into pretty boxes with tissue paper and ribbon would make a very special gift. Once the centres have been made, it is just a matter of immersing them in melted chocolate and carefully placing them down on paper to dry. Moulded chocolates are also easy to make by simply filling various shaped moulds. All sorts of decoration can be added: chocolate curls, cut-outs, crystallized petals and flowers. Alternatively, simply pipe chocolate designs onto the surface of each chocolate.

Nut clusters, fudge chocolate sweetmeats and praline crunch are quickly made and always popular. When entertaining, the perfect final touch to a dinner party would be to serve a plate of chocolate petit fours. The delicate peppermint bubbles just melt in your mouth; or for a more sophisticated flavour, serve japonnaise fingers, macaroons or whole dipped fruits. The white chocolate truffle cups are an extravagance everyone will enjoy.

pieces and dry overnight in a warm place.
Brush marzipan lengths with melted
chocolate and cut into ½" (1cm) slices.

Have bowls of various melted chocolate
ready, and a paper-lined tray. Using a fork,
dip fondants and other centres into
chocolate, tap to remove excess and place
on tray.

Repeat for all centres. Leave plain or
mark tops with a fork, or decorate with
crystallized petals and mimosa balls. Leave
to set. Pipe threads of contrasting chocolate
over remaining plain chocolates, if liked.

WHITE TRUFFLED CUPS

Makes 20

6 pistachio nuts,
  skinned and chopped

8oz (225g) white
  chocolate, melted
1oz (25g) unsalted
  butter, softened
1 tbsp whipping cream
1 tbsp kirsch

Place 20 foil sweet cases on a tray. Brush inside of each to coat evenly using ½ white chocolate. Chill.

Add butter, cream and kirsch to remaining chocolate; stir until well blended. Cool, stirring occasionally, until mixture peaks softly.

Pipe swirls of chocolate mixture into each chocolate case. Sprinkle with pistachio nuts and leave to set. Peel off foil cases if desired.

CREAMY CHOCOLATE FUDGE

Makes 64

1 lb (450g) granulated
   sugar
1/2pt (300ml) double
   cream
2oz (50g) unsalted
   butter

3 tbsp water
1/4pt (150ml) milk
8oz (225g) plain, milk
   or white chocolate
   pieces

In a large thick-based pan, place all ingredients except chocolate. Stir occasionally over gentle heat until completely dissolved.

Stir in chocolate; when melted, boil steadily, giving an occasional stir, until soft ball stage is reached (238°F/114°C on sugar thermometer).

Remove pan from heat and beat until mixture just begins to thicken. Pour into a buttered 8" (20cm) tin and leave to set.

Mark and cut into 1" (2.5cm) squares.

JAPONNAISE FINGERS

Makes 30

1 egg white
2oz (50g) caster sugar
1½oz (40g) ground almonds
1oz (25g) milk chocolate, melted

Whisk egg white until stiff, then gradually whisk in sugar until thick. Fold in almonds until evenly blended.

Using a ½" (1cm) plain nozzle, pipe 30 1½" (4cm) lengths of mixture, a little apart, on a bakewell-lined baking sheet.

Bake in a preheated 275°F/140°C/Gas 1 oven for ½ hour until firm. Cool on bakewell.

Dip each finger diagonally into melted chocolate, and leave on bakewell to set.

FRUIT AND NUT CLUSTERS

Makes 30

2oz (50g) hazelnuts,
   toasted and chopped
2oz (50g) glacé
   cherries, chopped
3oz (75g) raisins
1oz (25g) candied peel,
   chopped
1 tbsp sherry
6oz (175g) plain eating
   chocolate, melted
icing sugar to dust

Mix hazelnuts, cherries, raisins, peel and
sherry together. Add chocolate and stir
until well blended.

Place 30 heaps of mixture on a bakewell-
lined tray. Leave to set, then dust lightly with
icing sugar.

PRALINE CHOCOLATE CRUNCH

Makes 36

4oz (100g) peanut
  kernels
8oz (225g) granulated
  sugar
2½floz (65ml) water

2oz (50g) milk eating
  chocolate, melted
2oz (50g) white
  chocolate, melted
2oz (50g) plain eating
  chocolate, melted

Place peanuts on a tray and warm in oven or under a grill.

Put sugar and water in a pan over gentle heat; stir occasionally until dissolved. Boil rapidly until syrup turns golden brown, remove from heat, add peanuts and pour mixture onto a bakewell-lined baking sheet.

As it sets, pull into 36 bite-sized pieces of praline, then leave until cold. Dip ⅓ praline into milk chocolate, ⅓ into white and rest into plain chocolate. Set on bakewell.

CHOCOLATE MACAROONS

Makes 30

2oz (50g) ground almonds
2oz (50g) caster sugar
I tsp cocoa
¼ tsp almond essence
I egg white, whisked
½oz (15g) flaked almonds
icing sugar to dust

Mix almonds, sugar and essence together. Stir in enough of egg white to form a soft piping consistency.

Using a ½" (1cm) plain nozzle, pipe 30 tiny rounds of mixture onto a bakewell-lined baking sheet.

Press a flaked almond on each and bake in a preheated 325°F/170°C/Gas 3 oven for 10–15 minutes until firm. Cool on bakewell. Dust with icing sugar.

135

CHOCOLATE DIPPED SWEETMEATS

Makes 30

3oz (75g) dried prunes,
  stoned
3oz (75g) dried dates,
  chopped
4oz (100g) dried
  apricots
4oz (100g) dried
  peaches
2 tbsp lemon juice
2oz (50g) plain
  chocolate, melted
2oz (50g) white
  chocolate, melted

Pass dried fruits through a coarse mincer
or chop coarsely in a food processor.
  Add lemon juice and mix together. Shape
into 30 small balls.
  Roll ½ in plain chocolate and remainder
in white chocolate.

FRUIT PETITS FOURS

Makes 48

6 dried prunes, stoned
6 dried whole dates,
  stoned
6 dried apricots
3 dried figs
2oz (50g) white
  chocolate, melted
½oz (15g) pistachio
  nuts, finely chopped

Cut prunes and dates in half, remove stones; halve apricots and cut figs into 4 slices.

Dip ½ each fruit into melted chocolate and place on a bakewell-lined tray. Sprinkle chocolate end with pistachio nuts and leave to set.

CHOCOLATE-DIPPED FRUITS

Makes 48

12 kumquats
6 green grapes
6 black grapes
12 cherries
12 small strawberries

12 raspberries
2oz (50g) white
  chocolate, melted
2oz (50g) plain eating
  chocolate, melted
2oz (50g) milk eating
  chocolate, melted

Wipe all fruit except strawberries and raspberries carefully with kitchen paper. Ensure surfaces are dry and clean. Leave all hulls and stalks intact.

    Taking 1 fruit at a time, hold by stalk or hull and dip ends into white, plain or milk chocolate. Place on bakewell to set. Keep cool until needed.

138

PEPPERMINT BUBBLES

Makes 30

1 egg white
2oz (50g) caster sugar
1/2 tsp creme de menthe
1oz (25g) chocolate
*   mint sticks, finely*
*   chopped*
cocoa to sprinkle

Whisk egg white until stiff, then
gradually whisk in sugar and creme de
menthe until thick. Fold 3/4 mint sticks in
carefully.

Place 30 tsp mixture on a bakewell-lined
baking sheet. Sprinkle each with remaining
mint sticks.

Bake in a preheated oven on lowest
setting for 1 hour or until crisp. Cool and
sprinkle with cocoa.

Novelties

Creative chocolate decorations and gifts, these art works in chocolate are fun to make and eat.

There are many events during the year when novelty food is appreciated. The obvious celebrations that spring to mind are Christmas and Easter, but other occasions such as Mother's Day, St. Valentine's Day and birthdays can become extra-special with chocolate gifts and decorations.

At Christmas time it is great fun to involve the family in making chocolate novelty decorations and biscuits to hang from the Christmas tree or to give as extra presents. Use any prettily shaped mould or cutter to make a variety of coloured chocolate novelties. Use the recipe ideas given here as a guide, and use your own imagination and skill to create something really different.

Tiny Easter eggs are pretty and really easy to make as long as the moulds are spotlessly clean. Build up the layers of chocolate to produce thicker shelled eggs, which are easier to handle. Fill them with special tiny gifts and decorate them with ribbons, flowers or chocolate piping.

Chocolate run-outs, curls, cut-outs and leaves add finishing touches to ice cream, small cakes, desserts, sweets and pastries. Make in advance and store in a cool place, so they can be used at a minute's notice.

CHOCOLATE CHRISTMAS PUDDINGS

Makes 12

12 chocolate truffles
(p.126)
6oz (175g) white
chocolate, melted
red and green oil-based
or powder food
colourings

Make chocolate truffles and coat in cocoa and icing sugar (p.126).

Use ½ chocolate to make chocolate cut-outs (p.149). Cut out 12 1" (2.5cm) rounds using a plain or fancy cutter.

Colour 1 tsp chocolate red and place in a paper piping bag.

Colour ½ remaining chocolate green and spread onto bakewell. When set, cut out 36 leaves using a holly cutter. Mark on veins with a knife.

Attach truffles onto chocolate rounds ('plates') with melted chocolate. Spoon some white chocolate over each truffle and decorate with 3 holly leaves. Pipe on a few red berries.

CHOCOLATE CURLS

*plain, milk or white
  confectioner's or
  baker's chocolate,
  melted*

Pour melted chocolate onto a rigid
surface such as marble, wood or plastic
laminate. Spread evenly backwards and
forwards with a palette knife until smooth.

When chocolate has set, but not hard,
use a sharp knife held at 45° angle to
chocolate. Draw knife across surface to
shave off thin layers of chocolate that form
into curls. To make large curls (or caraque),
draw knife down whole length of chocolate.

Make chocolate shavings in same way but
let chocolate set a little harder, and draw
knife only half-way across surface to make
half-curls.

To make tiny curls, use a potato peeler to
shave curls off a block of chocolate, or grate
on a coarse grater.

CHOCOLATE HEARTS

Makes 5

8oz (225g) white
chocolate, melted

2oz (50g) plain
chocolate, melted
thin ribbon

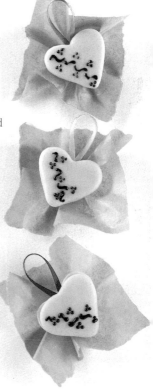

Using a 1½" (4cm) heart-shaped
template, draw around shape 10 times
on bakewell. Invert paper.

Pipe a fine outline of white chocolate
around heart shapes. Fill centre of each
heart with chocolate until they look rounded
and over-full. Leave to set hard.

Peel off each heart. Pipe plain chocolate
designs onto 5 hearts. When set, sandwich
with undecorated hearts using a little
chocolate, and placing a ribbon loop in-
between. Press gently together and leave to
set in fridge for ½ hour.

Wrap in cling film or hang up for
decorations. *Note*: For single hearts, place
loop in position while filling in centre.

CHOCOLATE RUN-OUTS

Chocolate run-outs are useful as a pre-made decoration, suitable for all types of cakes and desserts or for hanging novelties at Christmas time. Once made, they can be stored for several weeks before using in an airtight box.

Run-outs are quite fragile to make, so it is best to choose solid shapes to start with and try more adventurous shapes once you master the skill. Start with things like letters, numbers, hearts and bells, and then go on to the more delicate run-outs. Always make extra to allow for breakages.

Choose your design (or use an appropriately shaped cookie cutter), and draw or trace accurately onto bakewell. Trace in the details and invert paper; stick down the edges.

Use fresh chocolate for run-outs, taking care not to overheat it when melting. Try to work on a day that is dry; humid weather can affect the chocolate when it sets, causing it to be dull, speckly or covered with a fat bloom.

Fill a greaseproof paper piping bag with chocolate, and snip off the point. Pipe around the outline of the design in one continuous thread, starting and finishing at the least noticeable point. Fill in, working from edges to centre, so that it looks over-full and rounded (it will shrink on drying). Allow to set in a cool, dry place, leaving attached to paper until required.

CHOCOLATE LEAVES

*rose, fruit or geranium
  leaves*
*white, plain or milk
  chocolate, melted*

Choose real leaves that are small and have well-defined veins, from flowers, herbs and fruits. Leave a small stem on each leaf if possible. Wash and dry thoroughly before using.

Using a medium-sized paint brush, thickly coat the underside of each leaf with melted chocolate, taking care not to paint over edge of leaves.

Leave to set on bakewell, chocolate side up, in a cool place. Just before using, peel leaves away from chocolate. Use for decorations.

CHOCOLATE CUT-OUTS

*milk, plain or white
  chocolate, melted*

Pour melted chocolate onto bakewell. Spread as evenly as possible with a palette knife.

Pick up corners of paper and drop a few times to level and remove air bubbles from chocolate.

When chocolate can be touched without sticking to fingers, place another piece of paper over top. Turn whole sheet of chocolate over, then peel off backing paper.

To cut out shapes, use any shaped cocktail, biscuit, plain or fluted cutter. Press onto chocolate, cut out and removes shapes.

To cut out squares or triangles, carefully measure and mark size of squares required. Using a fine sharp knife or scalpel and a straight edge or ruler, cut along marked lines and remove shapes. Cut in half diagonally for triangles. Leave in a cool place to set hard.

MOULDED ANIMALS

Makes 1 medium,
2 small or 4 tiny

4oz (100g) white, plain
or milk chocolate,
melted
ribbon

Using a double shape, ensure inside
is perfectly clean by polishing with
cotton wool.

Half-fill each mould with melted
chocolate, swirling to coat inside evenly.
Pour out excess and draw a knife across top
of mould to neaten edges. For solid shapes
fill moulds completely. Invert onto bakewell
and leave to set.

Repeat process to give 3 layers of
chocolate in mould. Leave to set hard.

Carefully release shapes from moulds by
pressing tops. Join both halves together with
melted chocolate, securing a ribbon loop
between halves for decoration

NOVELTY BISCUITS

1 quantity biscuit dough (p.33)
8oz (225g) white chocolate, melted
assorted oil-based or powder food colourings
pretty ribbons

Roll and cut out biscuit dough into assorted shapes using biscuit cutters. Make a hole at top of each and bake according to recipe (p.33). Cool.

Divide chocolate into batches. Keep one plain and colour remainder with food colourings.

Spread some biscuits with white chocolate and leave to set. Pipe lines, dots or swirls of coloured chocolate onto all biscuits to decorate, and leave to set hard. Thread ribbon through each, hang up as decorations or wrap in cling film for gifts.

CHOCOLATE EASTER EGGS

Makes 3

8oz (225g) plain, milk
or white chocolate,
melted
chocolate rose leaves
(p.148)
sugar-frosted flowers
pretty ribbon

Polish inside of 6 small Easter egg moulds to ensure they are clean.

Fill each mould with melted chocolate, leave in a cool place for a few minutes, then pour excess chocolate back into bowl. Draw a palette knife across top of moulds to neaten.

Invert moulds onto bakewell and leave until set. Repeat process of filling and setting to give 3 layers. (To make solid eggs fill moulds completely.) Leave to set hard.

Carefully release eggs from moulds by pressing tops. Join both shells together with melted chocolate. Rest on an upturned egg box.

Decorate with piped chocolate around join, chocolate leaves, frosted flowers and ribbons.

Cook's Note: To make sugar-frosted flowers, choose fresh, simple small flowers such as violets, primroses, tiny daffodils, freesia or fuschias. Dry flowers with kitchen paper, leaving a small stem if possible. Brush both sides of flower with lightly beaten egg white. Spoon caster sugar over flowers to coat evenly, then carefully shake to remove excess. Leave to dry on kitchen paper in a warm place.

PIPED CHOCOLATE PIECES

white, plain or milk chocolate, melted

Draw chosen designs onto a piece of paper. Place wax paper over top and secure corners down with tape.

Fill a greaseproof paper piping bag with chocolate, fold down top and snip point off end. Pipe fine threads of chocolate following designs. Leave to set, then carefully slide a thin palette knife under each piece to release. Use to decorate cakes, sweets and desserts.

SIMPLE CHOCOLATE DECORATIONS

*white, plain or milk
chocolate, melted
assorted oil-based or
powder food
colourings
pretty ribbons*

Use any plastic novelty moulds such as Christmas tree ornaments, animals, leaves or flowers.

Divide white chocolate into batches and colour with different food colourings, keeping one plain if liked. Fill moulds with the coloured, white, plain or milk chocolate, and leave until slightly set.

Place a ribbon loop into some as required and set hard. Press to turn out.

TINY CHOCOLATE BOX

4oz (100g) white, plain or milk chocolate, melted

2oz (50g) white or plain chocolate (contrasting with above), melted

Following instructions for chocolate cut-outs (p.149), spread chocolate and cut into following shapes: Base and lid, cut two 1¾" (4.5cm) squares. Side pieces, cut four 1½" (4cm) squares. (Or, cut out shapes to make size of box required.)

Using a ¼"/5mm cutter, cut out 5 rounds for feet and knob.

To assemble: taking one piece at a time, brush base and edges of side pieces and stand on base to form a box. Trim base and lid to fit sides with a sharp knife. Stick feet

in position underneath box and knob on
top of lid.

Using contrasting chocolate, pipe small
dots around joins, piping patterns onto sides
if liked (or, attach small moulded chocolate
shapes or sugar-frosted flowers). Leave to
set hard.

Fill with home-made chocolates
(pp.125–139) or sugar-frosted flowers (p.153)
and rest lid on top.

INDEX

ACKNOWLEDGEMENTS

My grateful thanks go to Mavis for her unfailing ability to type my copy at all hours, and to my recipe tasters Emma, Anna, Yolanda, Bunny, Sandy and Audrey for their invaluable comments. I also thank Muffy for her beautiful ribbons and Alan for his patience, and all the people who contributed their efforts to this book.